WAR AND THE LIBERAL CONSCIENCE

In Memoriam

Edith Howard 1891–1977

MICHAEL HOWARD

War and the Liberal Conscience

Columbia University Press
New York

Columbia University Press
Publishers Since 1893
New York

Copyright © Michael Howard, 2008
All rights reserved

Library of Congress Cataloging-in-Publication Data

Howard, Michael Eliot, 1922–
  War and the liberal conscience / Michael Howard.
    p. cm.
  Includes index.
  ISBN 978-0-231-70048-1 (pbk. : alk. paper)
  1. Peace—History—20th century. 2. World politics—To 1900. 3. World politics—20th century. 4. War—History—20th century. 5. Liberalism. 6. Europe—Politics and government. I. Title.

JZ5560.H75 2008
303.6'6—dc22

2007044192

∞
Columbia University Press books are printed on permanent and durable acid-free paper.
This book is printed on paper with recycled content.
Printed in India

p 10 9 8 7 6 5 4 3 2 1

References to Internet Web sites (URLs) were accurate at the time of writing.
Neither the author nor Columbia University Press is responsible for URLs
that may have expired or changed since the manuscript was prepared.

CONTENTS

Foreword to the 2008 Edition	vi
Introduction: George Macaulay Trevelyan	1
1. The Growth of the Liberal Conscience 1500-1792	5
2. War, Peace and Nationalism 1789-1870	23
3. The Coming of the First World War 1870-1914	43
4. Arms and the Covenant 1914-1935	63
5. The Challenge of Fascism 1936-1945	83
6. The Challenge of Communism 1945-1975	101
Index	121

Foreword

All histories bear the imprint of the time that they are written. The lectures from which this book is derived were delivered in 1977, when the United States was still recovering from the trauma of the war in Vietnam. She had entered that war in the belief that she was fighting to defend the Free World—that is, a world governed by the values of liberal democracy—against the incursions of totalitarian tyranny. She ended with the awful suspicion that America herself was now suppressing a people struggling to be free. It was partly a perception of this tragic dilemma that led me to tackle this subject in the first place.

The book was reprinted in 1989, on the eve of the end of the Cold War. The Soviet Union had not yet collapsed, but under Ronald Reagan the United States had recovered its self-confidence, rebuilt its military strength, and again proclaimed herself ready to use her power to protect or extend liberty wherever it might be threatened. But among her policy-makers, there now raged a three-cornered debate. There were the 'classical' liberals whose pedigree is traced in the earlier chapters of this work. The descendants of Tom Paine and Jeremy Bentham, they believed that peace could be established by the replacement of the old aristocratic order, with its belief in the Balance of Power, by democratic nations freely co-operating under the banner of the United Nations; a school embodied in the person of President Jimmy Carter. Secondly there were the 'realists', led by Dr Henry Kissinger, who believed, to the contrary, that peace was best preserved by accepting and preserving that very balance between powers, whatever their internal governance, that the liberals considered anathema. Finally there was emerging a school that might be called 'muscular liberalism' but oddly adopted the label of 'neo-conservative', who believed that the United States should not hesitate to unilaterally use her enormous strength to destroy the enemies of the Free World wherever they showed themselves, and need not be too nice about the methods she used or the allies she co-opted—or abandoned—in the process. It was a policy identified, rightly or wrongly, with the regime of President Ronald Reagan. Certainly the fact that the Soviet Union collapsed on his watch and the Cold War ended in total and bloodless triumph seemed to vindicate the neo-conservative creed.

Two further decades have now passed, which saw the revival of something like classical liberalism under President Clinton and the elder President Bush, when the United States co-operated with allies and former adversaries, under the aegis of the United Nations, in maintaining 'collective security' and using force only if necessary to do so. But then came the shock of 9/11, and the revelation that the United States had enemies who could inflict terrible damage on her people and be neither deterred nor defeated by traditional means. At the same time the power and reach of America's armed forces was unsurpassed in the history of mankind. Given these circumstances the neo-conservatives were able to argue persuasively that American policy need no longer be shackled by the alliances and constraints involving both a 'realist' policy of bargaining with adversaries or a liberal one of international co-operation. America would fight her own 'War against Terror'.

The war in Iraq was the result. At the moment of writing it has not yet ended.

'History' does not repeat itself, but events sometimes significantly recur. Readers will find on these pages the words used by Gladstone, the very embodiment of 'the liberal conscience', to justify Britain's unilateral invasion of Egypt in 1882:

> 'We should not fully discharge our duty if we did not endeavour to convert the present state of Egypt from anarchy and conflict to peace and order. We shall look... to the co-operation of the Powers of civilised Europe. But if every chance of obtaining co-operation is exhausted, the work will be undertaken by the single power of England.'

It was. The campaign was brief and comparatively bloodless. But in order to convert Egypt 'from anarchy and conflict to peace and order', the British found it necessary to remain for another seventy years.

Sadly little seems to have changed, either in the aspirations of the liberal conscience, or in their unintended results.

November 2007   Michael Howard.

INTRODUCTION

George Macaulay Trevelyan

If one were to play a game of 'free association' with the name of George Macaulay Trevelyan, in whose honour these lectures were originally delivered, one of the first ideas that comes to mind would most certainly be the vague but splendid concept of Liberalism. Trevelyan was the last of the great Victorian liberal historians—perhaps the last of the great Victorian liberals. For him history really was the tale of freedom broadening down from precedent to precedent. For him the seventeenth century was the era when Englishmen burst the bonds of monarchical tyranny, as the United States was to burst them a hundred years later; and the nineteenth century was the age when the people of Europe, pre-eminently the Italians, came to share the blessings of freedom and nationhood in their turn. After that everything went wrong. 'I do not understand the age we live in', he wrote in a private letter in 1926,[1] 'and what I do understand I do not like.' The signposts of the past as he understood it bore little relevance to the deepening confusion of the present. Other liberals, notably his brother Charles, who will figure largely in the following pages, strode boldly forward into the new age under the banner of socialism, seeing in the confusion of their times only new challenges and new opportunities for the old ideals. George Macaulay Trev-

---

1 Transcribed by the Right Hon. The Lord Trevelyan K.G. in his unpublished memoir on the Trevelyan family, to which I am indebted for other family details.

elyan watched with puzzled sympathy, but could not bring himself to join them.

Closely associated with the concept of Liberalism, in our image of George Trevelyan, would be that of War. Trevelyan was that not uncommon phenomenon, a profoundly pacific and kindly man with a passionate interest in military affairs. The floor of the family home in Northumberland was laid out with a vast war game to which the Trevelyan brothers devoted themselves whenever they had the opportunity. The two great trilogies on which Trevelyan's reputation rests, his study of Garibaldi and his work on *England under Queen Anne*,[2] were pre-eminently military histories in which lavish descriptions of military operations enjoyed pride of place. He had none of our contemporary inhibitions about writing 'drum and trumpet history'. War for him was the very stuff of history, and he found no difficulty in reconciling it with his Liberalism. How have men gained and preserved their liberties, he would have asked, except by fighting? John Bright, the peaceful (though by no means pacifist) Quaker, was one of his heroes, but Garibaldi was another, and he saw no conflict between the two. Nor indeed did they. Bright's journals report Garibaldi greeting him and his Quaker colleagues when he visited England with the words 'I am of your principles, for I am a soldier and I am a soldier of peace'.[3] He was not the last 'freedom-fighter' to make such a claim.

As a young man Trevelyan set himself against the militant imperialism of the Joseph Chamberlain era, and opposed the Boer War. He was, oddly enough, prominent as a 'pro-Boer' while his brother Charles was flirting with Liberal Imperialism. In 1914 the roles were to be reversed. Charles resigned his ministerial post at the Board of Education in protest against Britain's declaration of war. He helped to found the Union for Democratic Control; he laboured unceasingly for a negotiated peace with Germany, and in 1918 he joined the Labour Party; informing his brother Robert that 'the only way

---

2   Garibldi's *Defence of the Roman Republic* (London 1907). *Garibaldi and the Thousand* (London 1909). *Garibaldi and the Making of Italy* (London 1911). *England under Queen Anne*, 3 vols (London 1930-34).

3   Quoted in G.M. Trevelyan, *John Bright* (London 1913) p.332.

to internationalism is through revolution... it is only through unity among the socialists of the world that internationalism can begin.'[4] It was a course which was to lead him to the far Left of the Labour Party and indeed beyond it. In 1939, together with Stafford Cripps and Aneurin Bevan, he was to be expelled from the Party for his continued advocacy of the Popular Front with the Communists. But his brother George had no qualms about the Great War. This conflict was not, he wrote to Charles, simply another manifestation of upper-class militarism such as Bright had attacked in the Crimea and he had himself opposed in South Africa. 'This war,' he told himself, 'is life and death.' He was to serve with gallantry and enthusiasm among his beloved Italians in what he saw as the last stage of the struggle for unity whose early history he had chronicled with such loving care.

The Trevelyan brothers can be seen as embodying two distinct traditions in the liberal philosophy about war and international relations, and it is with the development and interaction of these strands that this work will be concerned. Both have a long and honourable lineage and remain strong sources of inspiration today. I have chosen the term 'liberal conscience', for the word 'conscience' implies not simply a belief or an attitude but also an inner compulsion to act upon it. And by 'liberals' I mean in general all those thinkers who believe the world to be profoundly other than it should be, and who have faith in the power of human reason and human action to change it, so that the inner potential of all human beings can be more fully realised. This excludes on the one hand those conservatives who accept the world as it unalterably is and adjust to it with more or less of good grace; and on the other those disciples of Karl Marx and other determinists who see men as trapped in predicaments from which they can be rescued only by historical processes, which they may understand but are powerless to control. It is a definition which today would probably cover almost the entire range of political thinkers in Britain and the United States. But it was a doctrine which sprang from obscure roots and took many centuries to grow to its present maturity.

---

4   Trevelyan papers, loc. Cit.

1
THE GROWTH OF THE LIBERAL CONSCIENCE 1500-1792

It is likely that ever since the origins of human society, men—or at least some men, and most women—have intermittently lamented the existence of war, except among those societies which have been able to convert it to pure ritual or pure gain. But even those who saw it as evil normally considered it a necessary evil; one for which responsibility lay elsewhere, which was part of God's purpose for the world, or an indispensable activity in preserving or extending one's creed and culture. Such has been in general the position of the Christian Church throughout most of its history. Those Christians who found an unbridgeable gulf between their beliefs and the practices of society in this respect have been, ever since the days of Constantine, a small minority among their fellow believers. The teachings of the Gospels were sufficiently flexible for Christianity to become, and to remain for a thousand years, one of the great warrior religions of mankind. The teachings of the Church began to change only when society and social perceptions began to change around it; when the warrior society which had developed in Europe to survive the great incursions of the eighth and ninth centuries began to relax and diversify; when the arts of peace became possible and desirable; when war ceased to be a question of stark necessity for survival but rather a matter of cultural habit; and when the warrior elites ceased to be seen as indispensable protectors and were increasingly regarded as an oppressive nuisance.

Some of the earliest expressions of this critical attitude are to be found in the works of Erasmus at the beginning of the sixteenth century. Erasmus's diatribes against war contain many lamentations about its incidental horrors, which were not in themselves unusual. He did not himself have any significant experience of war. He did indeed write an account of a battle, a kind of literary parallel to Uccello's picture 'The Rout of San Romano', but this appears to have been based on a letter from a friend describing Henry VIII's expedition to France in 1512:

> ... The barbarous cohorts whose very faces and shouts strike terror to the heart; the iron-clad troops drawn up in a battle-array, the terrifying clash and flash of arms, the hateful noise and bustle of a great multitude, the threatening looks, harsh bugles, startling peal of trumpets, thunder of the bombards... a mad uproar, the furious shock of battle, and then wholesale butchery, the cruel face of the killers and the killed, the slaughtered lying in heaps, the fields running with gore, the rivers dyed with human blood...[1]

Erasmus' disgust at war in fact was probably provoked, as is so often the case, far more by a purely personal, emotional shock: the death of his beloved pupil Alexander, son of King James IV of Scotland, a beautiful, wise, learned young man who was killed with his father at the battle of Flodden: 'Tell me,' lamented Erasmus in his threnody, 'what had you to do with Mars, the stupidest of all the poet's gods, you who were consecrated to the Muses, nay to Christ? Your mouth, your beauty, your gentle nature, your honest mind—what had they to do with the flourishing of trumpets, the bombards, the swords?'[2]

'The *stupidest* of all the gods': that surely is a new note. War was stupid. It was irrational. It was neither glorious nor necessary. Those who conducted it were worthy not of admiration but of contempt. Erasmus despised the profession of arms with a scorn which generations of intellectuals were to inherit. 'Military idiots,' he called them, 'thick-headed lords... not even human except in appearance.' 'Among the soldiers,' he wrote bitterly, 'the one who has conducted himself with the most savagery is the one who is thought to be captain in the next war.'[3] Such a view went against the whole grain of contemporary

---

1 Desiderius Erasmus, *Dulce Bellum Inexpertis* in M.M. Phillips, ed., *Erasmus and His Times* (Cambridge 1967), p. 110.
2 *Spartam nactus es, hanc orna* in Phillips, op. cit., p. 105.
3 Ibid. p. 116-125.

culture. *Virtú*, the all-round excellence to which Renaissance Man aspired, displayed itself as much on the battlefield as in the study and boudoir, as Baldassare Castiglione's *Cortigiano* makes clear;[4] while more popular images of chivalry were still based on the romances of Malory, Ariosto and Amadis de Gaul.

Erasmus' attack on war was emotional rather than reasoned. 'There is nothing more wicked,' he wrote, 'more disastrous, more widely destructive, more deeply tenacious, more loathsome, in a word more unworthy of man, not to say a Christian.'[5] The priority is interesting. It is primarily on the grounds of *humanity* that Erasmus condemns war, not those of religion; in the same way he saw his pupil consecrated to the Muses, with Christ added almost as an afterthought. But he also developed rational arguments against war, which were later to become the commonplaces of liberal pacifism. Princes who wished to display their power and glory, suggested Erasmus, would be better employed developing the welfare of their own kingdoms rather than extending their boundaries at the price of untold suffering. War, he suggested, was 'unnatural': animals did not make war on one another. 'Whoever heard of a hundred thousand animals rushing together to butcher each other, as men do everywhere?'[6] It was a mask behind which governments could extend their powers over their subjects, since 'once war has been declared, then all the affairs of the State are at the mercy of the appetites of a few.'[7] Even 'just' wars he regarded as unacceptable, for reasons which are of continuing relevance. 'If a claim to possession is to be reckoned sufficient reason for going to war,' he wrote, 'then in such a disturbed state of human affairs, so full of change, there is no one who does not possess such a claim. What people has not, at one time or another, been driven out of its lands, or driven others out?' and were not the costs of defending even a righteous cause likely to be excessive? If you find, by balancing out one set of advantages and disadvantages with

---

4   See J.R. Hale, 'War and Public Opinion in Renaissance Italy' in E.F. Jacob, ed., *Italian Renaissance Studies* (London 1960).

5   Phillips, op. cit. p. 107.

6   Ibid. p. 112.

7   Ibid. p. 137.

another, that an unjust peace is preferable to a just war, why do you want to try the fortunes of Mars?'[8]

These are arguments which we will repeatedly meet again: war is both unnatural and irrational; it is a wasteful diversion of resources from welfare to destruction; it is engineered by governments for evil reasons of their own; even the most apparently laudable of ends can never justify the means involved. Erasmus did not concede, indeed, that there could be any circumstances under which war would be justified, and when one considers the nature of the wars being fought in the Europe of his time—the extravagant parades of Henry VIII and Francis I, the bellicose trumpeting of Pope Julius II—one can understand why. The medieval ideal, that force could be justly used only by Christian chivalry for the defence of Christendom and for the maintenance of God's justice within its borders, was virtually dead. The modern concept of force as a necessary instrument in preserving an orderly system of states was only beginning to appear—in the most shadowy of forms—in the work of Machiavelli. War in Europe at the dawn of the sixteenth century was largely a matter of competitive display of *virtù* in its most debased and ludicrous form.

Beyond these surface manifestations, with all their terrible consequences, Erasmus did not enquire. With all his genius he was not a profound political analyst, nor did he ever have to exercise the responsibilities of power. Rather he was the first in that long line of humanitarian thinkers for whom it was enough to chronicle the horrors of war in order to condemn it; men who may command one's instinctive agreement, but provide little constructive advice as to how to deal with the phenomenon which they find so abhorrent to nature and reason.

Very different was the approach of Erasmus' friend, Thomas More; a man who *had* exercised political responsibility and, perhaps in consequence, saw the problem in all its complexity.

More agreed with Erasmus that there was nothing in the least glorious about war. He tells us that the inhabitants of his ideal state, Utopia, 'hate and detest war as a thing manifestly brutal... Against the usage of almost all other nations they consider nothing so inglo-

---

8   Ibid. p. 131-2.

rious as the glory won in war.'[9] The Utopians went to war cautiously and reluctantly; but go to war they did, and for a wide variety of reasons. Most of these derived from concepts of *jus ad bellum*, widely current in the later Middle Ages; war to protect ones own territory or that of friends against invasion; 'to free some wretched people from tyrannous oppression and servitude'; 'to help friends, not only in defence, but in avenging injuries'. To these justifications, most of which one would have found in any medieval legal text, the Utopians added a startlingly new and relevant one: 'They account it a very just war if a people possess land that they leave idle and uncultivated and refuse the use and occupancy of it to others who according to the law of nature ought to be supported from it.'[10] Thus, while perpetuating the medieval concept of the 'just' war, More looked blandly forward to the colonial wars of the next three hundred years. But whatever their justification, wars should not, in More's view, be fought as men of the Renaissance fought them—at least those fought in Northern Europe. There was to be no glory in them, and as little blood should be shed as possible. War should be the continuation of policy, and with the minimal admixture of other means.

As a result, More has his Utopians conduct their wars with humane ruthlessness. They had, he said, 'this one aim in war, to accomplish what they would gladly have achieved without war if just terms had been granted in time.'[11] They set a premium, not on courage and honour, but on skill and cunning. They offered rewards for the assassination of enemy leaders. They fomented internal factions, and if that did not work 'then they arouse the neighbouring people against the enemy and induce them to revive some old claims, such as kings never lack.' If possible they used mercenaries rather than fought themselves; but if forced to it 'they join battle with a boldness as great as their prudence in avoiding it... Their skill in warfare increases their valour, and the sound ideas instilled into them in childhood by

---

[9] St. Thomas More, *Complete Works*, Edward Surtz and J.H. Hexter, ed. (Yale University Press 1965), vol. iv. pp. 201ff.

[10] Ibid. p. 137.

[11] Ibid. p. 203.

instruction and the wise institutions of the commonwealth add to their courage.'[12]

More was no less humane, not to say Christian, than Erasmus, but he understood that the horrors of war were not to be averted simply by complaining about them. He realised that war would be a problem even for Utopians. He accepted, as thinkers of the next two hundred years were to accept, that European society was organised in a system of states in which war was an inescapable process for the settlement of differences in the absence of any higher common jurisdiction. That being the case, it was a requirement of humanity, of religion and of common sense alike that those wars should be fought in such a manner as to cause as little damage as possible. Soon the details of this philosophy were to be fleshed out by the great international lawyers of the seventeenth and eighteenth centuries: Grotius, Pufendorf, and Eméric Vattel. For better or worse, war was an institution which could not be eliminated from the international system. All that could be done about it was, so far as possible, to codify its rationale and to civilise its means.[13]

Nearly two hundred years were thus to pass without any great outcry being made against the institution of war, and one may well wonder why. Perhaps on the continent of Europe scholars and men of letters were too dispirited by the black horrors sardonically chronicled by Grimmelshausen in *Simplius Simplicissimus*, while in England warfare was too much part of a lucrative process of competitive commercial expansion, fought very largely outside Europe, to arouse much humanitarian concern. But some voices rose above the clamour of the Thirty Years War. Grotius opened his *De Jure Belli ac Pacis* (1625) with a denunciation of the 'license in making war', which he observed all about him, 'of which even barbarous nations would have been ashamed.'[14] The French monk Eméric Crucé, whose *Nouveau Cynée* published in 1623 is remembered chiefly for its pioneer propos-

12 Ibid. p. 211.
13 See J.T. Johnson, *Ideology, Reason and the Limitation of War: Religious and Secular Concepts 1200-1740* (Princeton 1975), pp. 208-258.
14 Hugo Grotius, *De Jure Belli ac Pacis*, ed. William Whewell (Cambridge 1853) vol. 1, p. lix.

al for a United Nations Assembly to settle international differences by compulsory arbitration, went further. He denounced war in truly Erasmian terms. The life of warriors he considered to be unworthy of civilised peoples: 'We must abandon these barbaric habits and show mankind the way of humanity and true honour, that they may cease to live in so brutal a fashion.'[15] Like Erasmus, but unlike More and Grotius, he did not consider that there could ever be a just cause for war. Wars arose from the twin vices of arrogance and brutality: abandon those, he suggested, and wars would forever cease.

Crucé, however, had thought more deeply about the causation of war than this simplistic analysis might suggest. He was one of the first scholars to realise that the incidence of war might be connected with the structure of society, and that this structure might be changed. Wars occurred, he considered, because 'men, particularly men of war, are naturally impatient of repose'. The way to abolish them was therefore to alter the balance of the social structure by encouraging the peaceful occupations—agriculture, commerce, the mechanical and liberal arts. The 'warrior spirits', Crucé admitted, could probably not be eliminated altogether; but they could be put to service in a small professional army whose main function would be to make war on pirates and 'savages'. (As with Thomas More, the unfortunate inhabitants of the extra-European world were excluded from his irenical intentions.) Finally, these peaceful pursuits would be best encouraged by total freedom of trade. Peace would encourage trade; trade would nurture peace. 'Conditions of intercourse must everywhere be equal, above all in a universal peace, where it is a question of maintaining good intelligence with the whole of the world.'[16]

Here, for the first time, is sounded the note which was to dominate so much liberal thinking about war and peace during the following two centuries. Wars arose because of international misunderstandings, and because of the dominance of a warrior-class. The answer to both lay in free trade—trade which would increase the wealth and power of the peace-loving, productive sections of the population at

---

15 Quoted in Edmond Silberner, *La guere dans la pensee economique du XVI au XVIII siècles* (Paris 1939) p. 128.

16 Ibid. p. 133.

the expense of the war-orientated aristocracy, and which would bring men of different nations into constant contact with one another; contact which would make clear to all of them their fundamental community of interests.

Crucé thus saw in economic development, in what Adam Smith was later to describe as a 'hidden hand', the long-term solution to the problem of war. No more than Erasmus before him, or Cobden after him, did he appreciate the full extent of the difficulties inherent in the state-system itself—a system which might persist and give rise to conflicts, irrespective of the composition of the ruling classes in the units which composed it. More orthodox thinkers, even men of such genius as Francis Bacon and John Locke, took this so much for granted that they devoted little time in their works to discussing war as a moral problem. Both considered it to be an entirely rational activity in the absence of a common tribunal to which nations could appeal. 'Want of a common judge with authority puts all men in a state of nature', wrote Locke; 'force without right, upon a man's person, makes a state of war, both where there is, and is not, a common judge.' Since states were in a 'state of nature' with respect to one another, governments had not only the right, but the obligation to 'employ the force of the community... abroad to prevent and redress foreign injuries and secure the community from inroads and invasions.'[17]

By the beginning of the eighteenth century political thinkers in general saw war as a necessary evil arising from a social organisation which itself was necessary to keep in check yet greater evils. During the course of that century this view became subtly modified. War might well be the consequence of social organisation, but this was to be seen as a reason for condemning society; not for justifying war.

At the very beginning of *L'Esprit des Lois* (1750) Montesquieu made the point that war was *un-natural*, since, contrary to Thomas Hobbes' famous reconstruction of the pre-societal condition, man in a state of nature was too *timid* to make war. As an individual he was the most defenceless of all the animals. But 'as soon as man enters

---

17 John Locke, *An Essay Concerning the Original Extent, and End, of Civil Government*, Part II, Chap. 3, in Peter Laslett, ed. *Locke's Two Treaties of Government* (Cambridge 1960), p. 296. See also Richard H. Cox, *Locke on War and Peace* (Oxford 1960).

a state of society he loses the sense of his own weakness; equality ceases, and then commences the state of war. Each particular society begins to feel its strength, whence arises a state of war between different nations.'[18] Montesquieu himself accepted this as inevitable and drew much the same conclusions as had Thomas More: 'The law of nations is naturally founded on this principle, that different nations ought in time of peace to do one another all the good they can, and in time of war as little injury as possible without prejudicing their real interests.' The right of war was derived from necessity and strict justice, and 'If those who direct the conscience or Councils of princes do not abide by this maxim, the consequence is dreadful: when they proceed on arbitrary principles of glory, convenience and utility, torrents of blood overspread the earth.'[19]

Rousseau, however, in his fragment, *L'Etat de Guerre*,[20] pointed to a different conclusion. He agreed with Montesquieu that man was by nature peace-loving and timid, and that only habit and experience made it possible for him to fight at all: 'It is only after he is a citizen that he becomes a soldier.' War, Rousseau observed, was not a matter of impulsive hostility, but 'a permanent state which presupposed constant relations'. It was therefore possible only between public persons; that is, 'the moral being whom one calls 'the sovereign', which was brought into being by the social compact, and whose wishes bear the name of laws.'

But Rousseau did not accept that war could be controlled or abolished by any rational 'law of nations'. That could do little or nothing to mitigate the competitive striving for power inherent in the structure of the state-system. Even less did a solution lie in any international organisation of the type which the Abbé Saint Pierre had proposed after the War of Spanish Succession in his *Projet pour une Paix Perpetuelle*; which was little more than an attempt to freeze the status quo by a mutual security pact. Rousseau in his edition of

---

18 De Montesquieu, *The Spirit of the Laws*, trsl. by T. Nugent (New York 1949), I.2, p. 5.

19 Ibid. X.2, p. 134.

20 C. E. Vaughan, *Political Writings of J.J. Rousseau* (Oxford 1962), vol. I, pp. 293-306.

that work expounded St. Pierre's proposals with considerably more elegance than had its author and then demolished them with a few swift blows. It was no good, he said, putting forward proposals which ran counter to the perceived interests of every government in Europe.[21] The evil had to be tackled at its root—the social compact itself. 'If the social compact could be severed at a stroke, at once there would be no more war. At a stroke the State would be killed, without a single man having to die.' Nor would this lead to the chaos so much feared by Hobbes. 'The mistake of Hobbes and the philosophers,' maintained Rousseau, 'is to confuse natural men with the men they have under their eyes, and to transfer into one system a being who can subsist only in another.' War was a social evil; it could be cured only by severing the bonds which held society together.[22]

Rousseau was no doubt being sardonic in putting forward this solution, but it was one that has appealed to the optimistic or the desperate in every generation; although to the more conventional it seems comparable to a recipe for curing a man of acute sinus trouble by cutting off his head. Even if one accepts Rousseau's own arguments, whatever the pristine virtues of man may have been in a state of nature, they would not instantly reappear as good as new on the dissolution of social bonds which have, by his own account, confined and corrupted mankind since the origins of organised society. It was with precisely these imperfect creatures, whom Hobbes had 'under his eyes' and from whose imperfections he was generalising, that statesmen had to deal; and the capacity of such people to subsist in the 'natural' condition to which Rousseau proposed to return them was highly questionable. Like so many of Rousseau's more startling ideas, this is one that does not bear close examination; as he himself was no doubt the first to realise.

In his denunciation of the vested interests of governments, of princes and their ministers, Rousseau joined a mainstream of liberal thinking that was gathering momentum, particularly in France, throughout the eighteenth century. The idea that war arose not from

---

21 Jean-Jacques Rousseau, *Perpetual Peace*, trsl. by E.M. Nuttall (London 1927), p. 99.
22 Vaughan, op. cit. pp. 301-306.

any imperfect pattern of social relations but from the wilful machinations of statesmen and soldiers, princes and diplomats, had historical roots which, as we have seen, can be traced back at least to Erasmus. In France at the time of the Enlightenment it was becoming almost an intellectual orthodoxy, for two very obvious reasons.

In the first place, the *Tiers Etat*, the non-noble section of the population to which the bulk of the *philosophes* belonged, was a group still excluded from effective political power; certainly from the conduct of military policy and of foreign affairs. This was the last monopoly to be yielded by the court. It was also true that the patterns of behaviour, and to some extent the career opportunities, of the aristocracy were shaped by the acceptance, or the expectation, of war as a normal social phenomenon; and that war as it had developed in Europe since the middle of the seventeenth century was for this class little more than an agreeable and far from uncomfortable extension of their extraordinary life style.[23] It could be argued that the ruling classes of Europe had, since the Peace of Westphalia, been almost too successful in reducing the chaotic warfare of the early seventeenth century to rational order. From one point of view, the elaborate diplomatic protocol which had developed since the time of Louis XIV, the calculations of statecraft based on concepts of the balance of power, the wars conducted by increasingly professionalised armies who, when they were not fighting, maintained courteous intercourse with one another—all this might be seen, by those with recollections of what had gone before, as a triumph of reason, civilisation and order. But it could also be seen, by those who took no part in it, as a gruesome and unnecessary game with no purpose except to maintain the power, the prestige and the emoluments of the players. The *philosophes* did not rejoice that war had become so comparatively civilised an affair; they objected that anything so barbaric should have survived at all.

The second reason was that it was becoming increasingly clear that in the Europe of the eighteenth century, especially for France, war did not pay. Under Louis XIV Colbert had been able to argue convincingly that war, wealth and state power were almost synonymous.

---

23 E. G. Leonard, *L'armée et ses problémes au XVIII siécle* (Paris 1958).

English economists were to continue to argue to the same effect well into the eighteenth century while the Royal Navy smashed open the Spanish monopolies in the Caribbean and squeezed the French out of India and the West Indies. But Colbert's policy had antagonised Europe and resulted in twenty-five years of war, between 1689 and 1713, which had left France destitute. No wonder the French economists changed their tune. Even before Adam Smith and the Physiocrats published their famous treatises, the whole apparatus of mercantilism was coming under attack by writers such as Jean-François Melon (1675- 1738), Marquis D'Argenson (1694- 1757), and Ange Goudar (1720- 1791).[24]

The spirits of war and of commerce, insisted these thinkers, were mutually incompatible. No one could profit from wars except a few contractors and, of course, armaments manufacturers. Trade should be free, they argued, since economic rivalry was a powerful contributory cause of wars. By the mid-eighteenth century all the material was at hand to be put together by François Quesnay, Turgot, and the Physiocrats in France, by Adam Smith and his followers in England, into a comprehensive theory, which went something like this. The laws of nature dictated harmony and co-operation. Providence had linked mankind by a chain of reciprocal needs which made impossible *a priori* any clash of economic interests (what the Marxists were later to term 'False Consciousness') that led to conflict and war. It should therefore, urged Quesnay, be the object of good government to avoid all possible cause for war, to concentrate as exclusively as possible upon the production of wealth.[25]

But how could any such policy be expected so long as government remained in the hands of the war-making classes who perpetuated the life-style and perceptions of their feudal ancestors? Even Montesquieu qualified his analysis of war as a necessary consequence of man's social condition by the bold and unhistorical statement, 'The spirit of monarchy is war and enlargement of dominion: peace and moderation are the spirit of a republic.'[26] And in Prussia Immanuel

---

24 Silberner, *Pensée économique du XVI au XVIII siécle*, pp. 172- 180.
25 Silberner, op. cit. p. 196.
26 Montesquieu, op. cit., IX. 2, p. 127.

Kant was to lay it down in his *Perpetual Peace* (1795) as the first requirement for perpetual peace between states that 'The Civil Constitution shall in every State be Republican... [since] if the sanction of the citizens is necessary to decide whether there be a war or not, nothing is more natural than that they would think long before beginning such a terrible game'; whereas the Sovereign 'abates nothing of his feasts, sports, pleasure palaces or court festivities, etc. during the war, and can therefore declare war as a sort of pleasure on the slightest provocation.'[27]

Kant's views on war and peace were more subtle than this quotation would indicate, and it is impossible to do justice to them in a short paragraph. On the one hand he adopted a Hobbesian view of the state of nature, in contrast to that of Montesquieu. He held that 'the state of peace among men who live together is not a natural state; for the natural state is one of war, i.e. if not a state of open hostilities, still a continuous threat of such. *The state of peace must be established* (my italics).[28] On the other hand he believed that wars in themselves served the purpose, in the long run, of establishing such a state of peace; since

> ... through the excessive and never-realised preparations for them, through the want which hence every state even in the midst of peace must feel, nature drives man to make attempts at first quite inadequate, to leave the lawless state of savages and enter a league of nations; where each state, even the smallest, may expect his security and his rights—not from its own power or its own legal views, but alone from this great league of nations, from a united power, and from the decision according to laws adopted by the united will.[29]

For Kant, therefore, a 'hidden hand' was making use even of war itself to bring about eventual harmony, 'perpetual peace'. But he did not, as a result, consider war to be in any sense justifiable; on the contrary, he regarded it as the very antithesis of the moral law. The whole idea of a 'law of war' he held to be self-contradictory. Nor

---

27 Immanuel Kant, *Perpetual Peace: A Philosophical Proposal* (Grotius Society Publication No. 7, 1927), p. 25.
28 Ibid. p. 24.
29 Quoted in C.J. Friedrich, *Inevitable Peace* (Harvard University Press 1948), p. 30.

did the inevitability of war make it, in his view, acceptable; for since eternal peace was the highest good, 'it is', he wrote, 'our duty to act according to the idea of such an end (which reason commands) even if there is not the least probability that it can be achieved'. Indeed, he considered 'the general and continuous establishment of peace constitutes not only a part, but *the entire end purpose of a theory of rights within the limits of pure reason*' (my italics).[30] To Kant, therefore, to struggle for peace was in itself a moral absolute.

Kant thus saw the establishment of 'republican constitutions', or, as we would call them today, 'responsible governments', as an intrinsic part of the establishment of a 'state of peace'; a basis from which mankind could proceed not only to an international system of states reciprocally bound by law, but to an international society of which all men would be free citizens. Rousseau, however, adduced a further argument in favour of 'responsible government'—one which Erasmus had raised before him, though without drawing out the conclusions. 'All the business of kings,' he wrote in his commentary on the work of St. Pierre, 'or of those to whom they delegate their duties, is concerned with two objects alone; to extend their rule abroad or make it more absolute at home.' War was indispensable to them in consolidating their hold over their peoples; as a result, 'conquering princes make war at least as much on their subjects as their enemies.'[31] If it was true that the end of absolutism would mean the end of war, then the converse would also be the case. The abolition of war would strike such a mortal blow at the raison d'être and the controlling mechanism of governments that they could never be brought to consent it. Rousseau therefore saw no prospect of schemes such as St. Pierre's League of States becoming adopted except as the result of revolutions; 'and on this assumption,' he remarked dryly, 'which of us would venture to say whether this European League is more to be desired or feared?'[32]

So the idea of the economists, that wars arose from a failure to appreciate the underlying harmony of nature and so to legislate as to

---

30 Friedrich, op. cit., pp. 85-6.
31 Rousseau, *Perpetual Peace*, p. 105.
32 Ibid., p. 113.

give it full scope, merged easily into the view of the *philosophes*, that war was rooted in the vested interests of the ruling classes, of the aristocracy against the Third Estate, and that it would never disappear until those classes were overthrown. One of the most extreme and consistent members of this latter school was Marquis de Condorcet, who constantly reiterated the view that 'the people' were always peace loving, plunged only by the whim of their rulers into war. For this situation, he maintained, diplomats had to bear a primary responsibility. So far instead of preventing war, diplomats only provoked it. Diplomacy, according to one of his contemporaries, was 'an obscure art which hides itself in the folds of deceit, which fears to let itself be seen and believes it can succeed only in the darkness of mystery.'[33] Alliances, according to Condorcet, 'are the only means by which the rulers of states precipitate the people into wars from which they benefit either by covering up their mistakes or by carrying out their plots against freedom.'[34] In a new world governed by reason and morality, diplomacy would therefore be unnecessary.

Just such a new world was coming into being across the Atlantic. In 1781 John Adams, the ambassador of the United States at the court of her ally Louis XVI, informed the Foreign Minister, Vergennes, that 'the dignity of North America does not consist in diplomatic ceremonials or any of the subtleties of etiquette; it consists solely in reason, justice, truth, the rights of mankind and the interests of the nations of Europe.'[35] The dream of the philosophers seemed to have come true: here at last was a Republic which had cast monarchy and aristocracy to the winds and proposed to found its policy upon reason and peace. The fact that there would not have been such a Republic had it not been for a prolonged war, and that that war would probably not have been won without an alliance entered into by a French government guided strictly by those diplomatic principles which the *philosophes* so heartily condemned, does not appear at the time to have been found embarrassing by anybody.

---

33 Quoted in Felix Gilbert, *To the Farewell Address: Ideas of Early American Foreign Policy* (Princeton 1961), p. 61.
34 Ibid. p. 65.
35 Ibid. p. 67.

Perhaps the most eloquent European exposition of the belief that the United States of America would inaugurate a new world order, was set out by Thomas Paine in his pamphlet *The Rights of Man* (1791-2). 'Government on the old system', he wrote, 'is an assumption of power, for the aggrandisement of itself; on the new, a delegation of power for the common benefit of society. The former supports itself by keeping up a system of war; the latter promotes a system of peace, as the true means of enriching a nation.' Only across the Atlantic, he asserted, was this new system as yet to be found, and, 'What Athens was in miniature, America will be in magnitude. The one was the wonder of the Ancient World. The other is becoming the admiration of the present.'[36]

In *The Rights of Man* one finds a synthesis of all the ideas whose evolution we have traced in this chapter, put together with so much lucidity, so much force, that virtually every liberal or socialist who has written about foreign policy since has been able to provide little more than an echo of Paine's original philippic. The cause of the general poverty and wretchedness of mankind, argued Paine, following Quensnay, 'lies not in any natural defect in the principles of civilisation but in preventing those principles having a universal operation; the consequence of which is a perpetual system of war and expense that drains the country and defeats the general felicity of which civilisation is capable.'[37] The answer, he considered, following Adam Smith, lay in free trade: 'If commerce were permitted to act to the universal extent it is capable, it would extirpate the system of war, and produce a revolution in the uncivilised state of governments.'[38] The fault, he stated, following Rousseau, lay in

> .... the system of government on the old construction, [for] the animosity which Nations reciprocally entertain is nothing more than what the policy of each of their governments excited to keep up the spirit of the system. Each government accuses the other of perfidy, intrigue and ambition, as a means of heating the imagination of their respective Nations and incensing

---

36 Thomas Paine, *Collected Writings* (London 1894), vol. I, pp. 413, 424.
37 Ibid. p. 454.
38 Ibid. p. 456.

them to hostilities. Man is not the enemy of man but through the medium of a false system of government.[39]

The hope, Paine believed, following Montesquieu and Kant, lay in the institution of Republics. 'The instant the form of government was changed in France,' he wrote in 1791, 'the republican principles of peace and domestic prosperity and economy arose with the new government; and the same consequences would follow in the case of other nations'. A year later he believed that the dawn was breaking. 'There is a morning of reason rising upon man on the subject of government, that has not appeared before. As the barbarism of the present old governments expires, the moral condition of nations with respect to each other will be changed. Man will not be brought up with the savage idea of considering his species his enemy.'[40]

Within a few months of these words being published France and her neighbours plunged into twenty-five years of continuous and ferocious warfare, which aroused between the different nations of Europe a deeper hatred than anything else that had yet been seen. Whatever morning was being heralded by the French Revolution, it was certainly not that of Reason, let alone of peace.

---

39 Ibid., p. 388.
40 Ibid., p. 453.

2
WAR, PEACE AND NATIONALISM 1789–1870

By the end of the eighteenth century a complete liberal theory of international relations, of war and peace, had thus already developed. Tom Paine's synthesis of the views of the Enlightenment in *The Rights of Man* provided a gospel which was to be preached virtually without alteration by many Western liberals until our own day. According to this doctrine, mankind would naturally live in a state of perfect harmony if it were not for the vested interests of governments—of what William Cobbett was soon to term 'The Establishment'. The whole 'war system' was contrived to preserve the power and employment of princes, statesmen, soldiers, diplomats and armament manufacturers, and to bind their tyranny ever more firmly upon the necks of the people. Break the power of the Establishment, introduce a political system in which popular interests were truly represented, demolish all artificial barriers to international intercourse, and the whole nightmare would quickly disappear. International differences would be resolved by appropriate institutions as smoothly as domestic ones. Peace was therefore fundamentally a question of the establishment of democratic institutions throughout the world.

That such a belief could survive not only the revolutionary and Napoleonic wars and the subsequent struggles for 'national liberation' which disturbed Europe during the nineteenth century, but also the gigantic holocausts of the twentieth—a period during which the power of the old aristocratic establishment was progressively constricted where it was not totally destroyed, and when popular pressure upon and participation within governments steadily increased, all without noticeable reduction in the incidence of wars—is in itself a legitimate subject for the historian's attention. That it did survive was largely due to a process of diversification and adaptation.

The original view of the eighteenth-century *philosophes*, that international disputes could be settled without violence, by reasoned discussion and agreement between men of good will, has remained the basis of most liberal Western thinking about international relations. The view held by Tom Paine, that such reasoned discussion would be possible only after revolutions had destroyed the old systems of government and brought reasonable and disinterested men to power, was also to thrive with appropriate modifications, and remains today the basis of most socialist thinking about international politics, but during the nineteenth century there emerged a third variant of the liberal teaching. According to this view, peace between nations would be possible only when those nations fully and freely *existed*. It was a necessary condition of peace that 'the people'—naturally by definition peace-loving—should come first to self-consciousness through struggle. Before co-operation must come self-realisation, which meant an emphasis on diversity rather than on community. This process would involve just and necessary wars to make possible ultimate peace. The description attached to the red, black and gold of the German tricolour would be appropriate for all the new national flags: *durch Blut und Nacht zum Licht*. That is the attitude to war and international politics, which, by and large, is now adopted by many of the nations of the 'Third World', and is now the *rationale* behind struggles for 'national liberation'.

Let us first consider what happened to the first of these views; the belief that once the underlying laws binding men together by common interest were fully understood the problem of war would disappear. The most influential formulation of this doctrine was to be that of Jeremy Bentham, whose *Plan for a Universal and Perpetual Peace* appeared in 1789, on the eve of the French Revolution. Bentham saw the problem of war and peace purely in terms of sensible action by governments responding to the free expression of public opinion. Like so much that Bentham wrote, the work was smug, parochial and simplistic, making sweeping generalisations on the basis of minimal knowledge. The necessary condition, in his view, for a universal and perpetual peace was for Britain and France to stop fighting one another about colonies. If it were not for colonial rivalries, he asserted, Europe 'would have had no wars but for the feudal system, religious antipathy, the rage of conquest and the uncertainties of succession. Of these for causes, the first is happily extinct everywhere, the second and third almost everywhere—and at any rate in France and England the last might, if not already extinguished, be so with great ease.'[1] So if Britain and France abandoned their foreign dependencies, reduced their navies to police proportions, foreswore discrimination in their trade and abandoned all alliances, foundations would be laid for the establishment of universal and perpetual peace.

Bentham thus applied the general prescription of the *philosophes* to the particular case of his own country and devised a programme which was to become the foundation of the British liberal foreign policy until the eve of the First World War. Peace would come through the abandonment of colonial ambitions, through reduction of armaments, through freedom of trade, and through detachment from continental entanglements; to which Bentham added some pointed remarks about secret diplomacy, which were to remain an intrinsic part of the liberal creed. 'Secrecy in the operations of the Foreign Department in England ought not to be endured,' he wrote, 'being altogether useless and equally repugnant to the interests of liberty and peace'.[2] But he went on to make more constructive proposals which have a deservedly honoured place in all histories of internationalism. He recommended that a Common Court of Judicature should be set up for the decision of differences between the several nations. He doubted whether this court would need coercive powers, although 'there might perhaps be no harm in regulating as a last resort, the contingents to be furnished by the several states for enforcing [its] decrees...' The effective power of the court would consist in the publicity of its proceedings, which should be fully reported throughout every member state. 'The power of information and rea-

---

1 Jeremy Bentham, *A Plan for a Universal and Perpetual Peace* (Grotius Society Publications 1927), p. 25.
2 Ibid. p. 31.

son over error and ignorance is much greater and much surer than that of exhortation, and all the modes of rhetoric over selfishness and malevolence.'[3]

Bentham therefore proposed that the most efficacious way of enforcing the jurisdiction of the court would be 'by introducing into the instrument by which such a Court was instituted a clause guaranteeing the liberty of the Press in each State.'[4] There is nothing to indicate that Bentham appreciated either the fundamental nature of the problem which would be created by such invasions of the sovereign powers of governments, or the difficulties which would arise (difficulties with which we in our day are sadly familiar) if some states enjoyed freedom of the press and other did not. Underlying the ideas of Bentham and all his disciples was the assumption that all peoples, all nations, all cultures, were homogenous or could be made so.

This was a new form of cultural imperialism which was repeatedly to provoke violent and sometimes bloody reactions. Giuseppe Mazzini well expressed the irritation it was to arouse:

All these soi-disant cosmopolitans,... so soon as any question of action and therefore organisation arises, invariably seek to make the centre of the movement their own country or their own city. They do not destroy nationality, they only confiscate all other nationalities for their own benefit. [They carry] the assumption of a *permanent, exclusive* moral and intellectual *initiative*, which is quite as dangerous to those people weak enough to admit it, as any other form of usurpation.[5]

Bentham in fact wanted to turn everyone into Englishmen. His recipe for perpetual peace could be effective only if a degree of cultural and political homogeneity could be established which did not as yet exist and which many people considered highly undesirable. It is a problem to which we shall return.

There was another difficulty about Bentham's proposals. He was not an absolute pacifist, any more than were any of the other thinkers we consider in this study. All accepted the need for self-defence, the obligation of governments to provide some level of armed forces for

---

3   Ibid. p. 28.
4   Ibid. p. 31.
5   Joseph Mazzini, *Life and Works* (London 1890), vol. III, p. 10.

protection against invasion. Bentham's objections to war were purely utilitarian. For Britain at least, war no longer paid. But he agreed that there were still circumstances in which for some people it did pay. 'Conquests made by New Zealanders,' he admitted, 'have some sense in them.' So would conquests made by a modern despot on the continent of Europe: 'The new property, being contiguous, is laid on his old property,' wrote Bentham, a decade before Bonaparte began his career of conquest. 'The inhabitants, as many as he thinks fit to set his mark on, go to increase his armies; their substance, as much as he thinks fit to squeeze from them, goes into his own purse.'[6] By this criterion the wars not only of Bonaparte, but of Hitler, were perfectly rational. But how, in that case, could they have been checked by an international Court of Judicature? And why should such despots permit any outside body to decide what should or should not be published within their domains?

It might have been expected that the experience of the Napoleonic Wars would have discredited the ideas of Bentham and the *philosophes*. The destruction of the feudal 'establishment' and the advent of popular democracy in France, so far from ushering in a new era of peaceful co-operation, unchained a bellicose regime, which had inflicted on Europe the worst wars that the Continent had experienced for two hundred years. It is hardly surprising that in 1815 European statesmen should have seen the best hope of peace to lie in the reconstitution of exactly those diplomatic mechanisms and balances, those confidential understandings and assurances, which liberals believed to be one of the major causes of war. Yet the experiences of 1792 to 1815 led liberal thinkers in France and Britain, and to a growing extent in the Unites States, not to re-examine their diagnosis of the causes of war, but to intensify their search for a cure along the lines which had already become for them almost traditional.

It is indeed from the end of the Napoleonic Wars that one can date the beginning of what was to become known as 'the Peace Movement'; that is, the political organisation of the middle-class liberals on a transnational basis to secure, by education, agitation and propaganda, the abolition of war. The social historian has no difficulty in explaining

---

6 Bentham, op. cit. p. 37.

why this should have been so. These were the men whose wealth and influence were being rapidly expanded by the developments in industry and trade which were transforming Europe and North America. Within their own societies they had to struggle against the attitudes and interests of aristocratic, agrarian-based elites who still derived status—particularly east of the Rhine—from their obsolete warrior functions. Externally, war disturbed the flow of trade, cutting off manufacturers from markets and sources of raw material. Economic historians still have some difficulty in determining whether on balance the benefits which the Napoleonic Wars conferred on the British economy outweighed the disadvantages,[7] but there was now quite certainly a strong desire among British business men to consolidate in peace such advantages as had been gained. From among their ranks, and their peers in France and the United States, the Peace Movement was able to derive political and financial support.

There was, of course, no lack of intellectual muscle behind the movement. Among British economists the ideas of Adam Smith and Bentham, among Frenchmen the ideas of Quesnay and Turgot, were rapidly becoming orthodox. James Mill, a founding father of Utilitarianism, saw in war the greatest obstacle to that accumulation of wealth which alone could ensure the greatest happiness of the greatest number. 'In every country where industry is free and where men are secure in the enjoyment of what they acquire, the greatest improvement which the government can possibly receive is steady and enlightened aversion to war,' he wrote in 1808.[8] 'Nothing can compensate the destruction of war. The creative efforts of individuals can never equal its gigantic consumption, and the seeds of prosperity are eaten up.' The economist John McCulloch considered it to be the primary task of political economists to destroy the mercantilist fallacy that war could ever be economically advantageous. 'The greater part of the war of the last century,' he wrote in 1824, 'with the exception of those that grew out of the French Revolution, were waged for the purpose of preserving or acquiring some exclusive commercial

---

7   See e.g. Phyllis Deane, 'War and Industrialisation' in J.M. Winter, ed. *War and Economic Development* (Cambridge U. P. 1975).

8   James Mill, *Commerce Defended* (London 1808), pp. 120-121.

advantage. But does anyone suppose that these contests could have been carried on, at such infinite expense of blood and treasure, had the mass of the people known that their object was utterly unattainable?'[9] Two decades later, in 1848, John Stuart Mill was able to write almost as of a *fait accompli*: 'It is commerce which is rapidly rendering war obsolete, by strengthening and multiplying the personal interests which act in natural opposition to it. And it may be said without exaggeration that the great extent and rapid increase of international trade, in being the principal guarantee of the peace of the world, is the great permanent security for the uninterrupted progress of the ideas, the institutions, and the character of the human race.'[10]

The same ideas were increasingly popular beyond the Channel. There the French economist Jean-Baptiste Say was also emphasising the counter-productiveness of war; which came about only because bad ministers wished to make themselves indispensable, because governments sought to silence domestic discontent, because the military sought prestige and promotion and because of the false doctrines of mercantilism. 'War costs more than its expense,' he pointed out, 'it costs what it prevents from being earned.'[11] But like John Stuart Mill, Say believed war to be obsolescent:

Just because war has become much more costly now than it was formerly, it is impossible for governments to wage it without the consent of the public openly expressed or tacitly understood. This consent will be obtained with more and more difficulty as the masses among the nations gain a better understanding of their true interests.

Say also believed, as had Crucé two hundred years earlier, that as the producing classes, *'les industrieux'*, became increasingly influential in society, so the importance of the predatory military classes would decline. Governments formed of such men would pursue policies in-

---

9 John McCulloch, *A Discourse on the... Importance of Political Economy* (1824), pp. 85-86.
10 J. S. Mill, *Principles of Political Economy* (London 1848), p. 582. See comments on all these authors in Edmond Silberner, T*he Problem of War in 19th Century Economic Thought* (Princeton U. P.), pp. 42-66.
11 Silberner, op. cit. p. 72. Say's ideas were set out in his *Traite d'economie politique* as early as 1803, but were to be fully developed in his *Cours complet d'economie politique pratique* (1829).

spired solely by principles of international solidarity.[12] The belief that the producing classes were replacing the despoiling classes and that therefore peace would replace war—a belief soon to be embodied in the work of Auguste Comte and the Positivists—is to be found in the work of Frédéric Bastiat who, in the 1840s, in Edmond Silberner's words, 'summed up the wholly optimistic and enthusiastic social dream of one or two generations of economists.'[13] Bastiat considered that war arose from the desire to despoil the labour of others. In the long run production would replace despoliation, and it was the duty of political economy to show the way. 'Political economy shows that, even if we consider only victorious people, wars are always waged in the interests of the few and at the expense of the many. It is therefore sufficient that many realise this truth clearly. The weight of Public Opinion, which is as yet divided, will bear entirely on the scale of peace.'[14]

In the education of public opinion, then, in the spread of commerce, and the advent to power of those classes which derive their wealth from commerce, these liberal thinkers of the early nineteenth century saw the answer to the problem of war. It was in order to work on public opinion that the first peace movements were founded; but the initiative came from men whose objection to war was not so much utilitarian as moral.

The Society of Friends, or 'Quakers', founded in England by George Fox in the seventeenth century and rapidly spreading in the American colonies, was one of the few Christian sects to adhere unswervingly to the absolute pacifism of the pre-Augustinian Church. Until the end of the eighteenth century it was a creed that applied only to their own intricate network of families; but by the beginning of the nineteenth century those families—Frys, Cadburys, Lloyds, Gurneys, Foxes, Sturges—were becoming increasingly prosperous, influential, and politically active both in Britain and the United States, and a new strain of evangelism was beginning to inspire their activities.[15] The Napoleonic Wars, by providing them with the first

---

12 Ibid. p. 81-82.
13 Ibid. p. 92.
14 Ibid. p. 94.
15 Peter Brock, *Pacifism in Europe* (Princeton U. P. 1972), p. 339.

opportunity on a large scale for that war-relief which was to earn them such well-deserved fame, brought many of them into direct contact with war in Europe at its worse; and they began to regard war as an evil, not from which they should hold themselves aloof, but which it was their duty to extirpate entirely. They began to move boldly into the political arena, organising, lobbying and writing.

One of the most vigorous of the new school of Quaker propagandists was a young draper from Exeter, Jonathan Dymond. Dymond said nothing that had not been said before him by Tom Paine and others, but he said it with great power, making sharper and more rancorous the note of class war. Wars, he wrote in a pamphlet published 1823,[16] arose from callus indifference to human suffering; from national pride and irritability; from false ideas of glory; from self-interest of statesmen who had 'many purposes of subtle policy which makes wars convenient'; and from the vested interests of 'a countless hosts of commissaries and purveyors and agents and mechanics [who] commend a war because it fills their pockets.' (In short, a 'military-industrial complex'.) Further, war 'offers to the higher ranks of society a profession which unites gentility with profit, and which without the *vulgarity* of trade, maintains and enriches them... It is in this manner that much of the rank, of the influence, and of the wealth of a country becomes interested in the promotion of wars.' Dymond was not prepared to accept the legitimacy even of defensive wars. 'When nations are mutually exasperated and armies are levied, and battles are fought,' he pointed out, 'does not everyone know that with whatever motive of defence one party may have begun the contest, both in turn become aggressors?... If a war has once begun, it is vain to think of distinctions of aggression and defence.' There was, he concluded, 'no hope of an eradication of War but by an absolute and total abandonment of it.' And this became the objective of an increasing number of dedicated, hard-working men in the United States and Western Europe during the next hundred years.

The first Peace Society—the Society for the Promotion of Permanent and Universal Peace—was founded in London in 1816 by

---

16 Jonathan Dymond, 'War, its cause, consequences etc.', in *Essays on the Principles of Morality* (London 1823).

the Quaker William Allen. A similar society was founded simultaneously in the United States. Their terms of reference were purely Benthamite. The American Peace Society aimed 'to increase and promote the practice already begun of submitting national differences to amicable discussion and arbitration, and... of settling all national controversies by an appeal to reason, as becomes rational creatures... this shall be done by a Congress of Nations whose decrees shall be enforced by public opinion that rules the world... Then wars will cease.'[17] Their activities proliferated. An international Peace Convention met in London in 1843 with 292 British, 26 American and 6 Continental participants; mainly discussing how to develop their missionary activities, also stressing in their resolutions the advantages of Temperance as facilitating 'reasonableness' in time of crisis.[18] Five years later, in 1848, a Peace Congress met in Brussels, and thereafter such Congresses were convoked annually in a different European city; increasingly impressive affairs, gaining the respectful attention of governments, despatching and receiving fraternal delegates, passing eloquent resolutions in favour of disarmament, arbitration and the brotherhood of man. Then in 1854 came the Crimean War and the enterprise for the time being collapsed.[19]

Meanwhile the activities of the Peace Movement had been enriched and strengthened by those of the Free Trade Movement, and it is not always easy to distinguish between the two. The moralism of the first and the utilitarianism of the second very broadly overlapped. The great English political leader who united the two streams was Richard Cobden. For him they were 'one and the same cause.'[20] But his motives were briskly utilitarian. As his biographer John Morley said of him, 'it was from the political, and not from the religious or humanitarian side, that Cobden sought to arouse men to the criminality of war.'[21] Cobden himself put it in 1846, 'the present system

---

17 A.C.F. Beales, *The History of Peace* (London 1931), pp. 46-53. Brock, op. cit. p. 345.
18 Beales, op. cit. p. 67.
19 Beales, op. cit. p. 74-81.
20 W.H. Dawson, *Richard Cobden and Foreign Policy* (London 1926), p. 131.
21 John Morley, *The Life of Richard Cobden* (London 1881), vol. II, p. 70.

corrupts society, exhausts its wealth, raises up false gods for hero-worship, and fixes before the eyes of the rising generation a spurious if glittering standard of glory... If we can keep the world from actual war, and I trust railroads, steamboats, cheap postage and our own example in Free Trade will do that, a great impulse will from this time be given to social reforms.'[22] Cobden was not, as he was at frequent pains to point out, a pacifist. He agreed that some wars might be necessary, even beyond the strict requirement of self-defence.[23] As he explained in 1853 there were in the Peace Movement 'those who oppose all war, even in self-defence; those who do not go quite so far, and yet oppose wars on religious grounds in all cases but that of self-defence. And there are those for whom politico-economical and financial considerations are not only the advocates of peace, but also of a diminution of our costly war establishments. Among this latter class I confess I rank myself.'[24]

The utilitarian arguments against war used by Cobden and his colleague John Bright, their open appeal to the pockets of the middle classes, did not make them universally popular. 'Manchester Peace Goods,' punned *Punch* sardonically, 'there is but one Manchester and the whole world is its profit.' The *Manchester Guardian* denounced the 'mischievous notion that the honour and safety of England are less dear to a large and important community than the profit of their industry.'[25] Cobden was deliberately provocative: for that sacrosanct image of British greatness, the Royal Navy, he proposed, in his own words, to 'substitute the more homely but enduring maxim *Cheapness*, which will command commerce... The standing armies and navies—whilst they cannot possibly protect our commerce, while they add by the increase of taxation to the cost of our manufacturers and thus augment the difficulty of achieving the victory of 'cheap-

---

22 Morley, op. cit. vol. I, p. 411.
23 J.A. Hobson, *Richard Cobden: the International Man* (London 1918), p. 387.
24 Ibid. p. 94.
25 Donald Read, *Cobden and Bright* (London 1967), pp. 131, 136.

ness'—tend to deter rather than attract customers.'[26] But in his view, profit and peace went hand in hand:

Free Trade [he demanded rhetorically at Covent Garden in September 1843 at the height of the Anti-Corn Law campaign], What is it? Why, breaking down the barriers that separate nations; those barriers behind which nestle the feelings of pride, revenge, hatred and jealousy which every now and then break their bonds and deluge whole countries with blood; those feelings which nourish the poison of war and conquest, which assert that without conquest we can have no trade, which foster that lust for conquest and dominion which sends forth your warrior chiefs to sanction devastation through other lands. [27]

And in a memorable phrase he called for 'as little intercourse as possible between Governments, as much connection as possible between the nations of the world.'[28]

Cobden and Bright had little to add except oratorical passion to the denunciations of the ruling classes (with their vested interest in and their arcane manipulation of the balance of power), which were already commonplace among liberal thinkers; but they made them part of the common currency of political dialogue. 'This excessive love for "the balance of power",' cried Bright in his great philippic at Birmingham in October 1858, 'is neither more nor less than a gigantic system of outdoor relief for the aristocracy of Great Britain.'[29] Six years later when Palmerston abstained from the intervention on the Schleswig-Holstein crisis, which was to provoke the first war of German unification, Bright rejoiced 'that this foul idol, fouler than any heathen tribe ever worshipped, has at last been thrown down... it is not possible for the eye of humanity to scan the scroll upon which are recorded the sufferings which the balance of power has entitled upon this country.' In describing his speech in his biography of Bright, G.M. Trevelyan was to comment, 'The idol, having thus fallen in 1864, remained prostrate as Dagon during the Continental wars of 1866 and 1870, enabling England to wax into prosperity

---

26 Hobson, op. cit. p. 35.

27 Richard Cobden, *Speeches on Questions of Public Policy* (London 1870), vol. I, p. 79.

28 Hobson, op. cit. p.34.

29 G. M. Trevelyan, *John Bright* (London 1913), p. 274.

and peace... Whether or not in our own day the idol has been refurbished is a point of moment to us all.'³⁰ It was indeed. Trevelyan wrote on the eve of the First World War, at a moment when a Liberal Government was being forced by events into acknowledging the European balance of power, not as an idol to be worshipped, but as a system from which it could not escape.

For the foul idol of the balance of power, Cobden and Bright substituted the one true God, non-intervention in Continental affairs, particularly in the domestic concerns of other countries. Cobden saw non-intervention, together with disarmament, arbitration and free trade, as an essential plank of the peace platform.'³¹ He had always, he told Bright in 1846, 'had an instinctive monomania against this system of foreign interference, protocolling, diplomatising, etc.' he had frequently noted, 'how much unnecessary solicitude and alarm England devoted to the affairs of foreign countries: with how little knowledge we enter upon the task of regulating the concerns of other people; and how much better we might employ our energies at home.'³² He watched in particular the agitation on behalf of Italian independence, which commanded so much Liberal support, with a thoroughly jaundiced eye. 'The truth is,' he wrote in 1856, 'it must again be told the English public and the world that our aristocratic politicians make political capital out of the Italians, Poles, Circassians, etc. for purpose of their own, and not with an intent of promoting liberty anywhere. And this game will go on so long as the English public allow them to parade their sympathies for the grievances of foreigners instead of doing the work of liberty at home.'³³

In his belief that England would best be occupied in minding her own business Cobden probably reflected the views of a large number of his countrymen. It was a philosophy which had behind it a respectable ancestry, going back through William Cobbett to

---

30 Ibid.
31 Hobson, op. cit. p. 82.
32 Dawson, op. cit. p. 97.
33 Ibid. p. 100.

Charles James Fox.[34] Certainly, as the franchise widened, British statesmen showed an increasing reluctance to play a leading role in European affairs, or to intervene on behalf of far away peoples of which they knew nothing. But in other respects Cobden and Bright found themselves swimming against, and ultimately swept away by, a tide of popular opinion which cast very grave doubt on the central thesis of the entire liberal creed: that it was only the ruling classes that wanted war, and that 'the people,' if only they were allowed to speak for themselves, would opt enthusiastically for peace.

The experience of the Crimean War was an ominous one for the Peace Movement. Lord Aberdeen's government faced the prospect of war against the Russian Empire with great reluctance, but there was no doubt whatever about the enthusiasm of British public opinion, as expressed by every conduit open to it.[35] Cobden had received a hint of what to expect at the Great Exhibition of 1851, in that very temple of peace and prosperity—the Crystal Palace; where, on the appearance of the Duke of Wellington, whom he regarded as the embodiment of the martial aristocratic establishment, 'the frenzy of admiration and enthusiasm which took possession of a hundred thousand people of all classes was one of the most impressive lessons I had ever had of the real tendencies of the English character.'[36] Cobden could only explain this phenomenon by suggesting that somehow the entire English people had been infected with aristocratic vices; that, as he put it the following year, 'the aristocracy has converted the combativeness of the English race to its own sinister ends.'[37] Certainly he proved unable to infect public opinion with his own virtues. His protests, and those of Bright, against British policy were howled down in the House of Commons, in the Press, and at meeting after public meeting. Cobden and Bright were thus the first liberal leaders, and by no means the last, to discover that peace

---

34 Cf. A.J.P. Taylor, *The Trouble Makers* (London 1957), passim esp., pp. 28, 39.
35 See Olive Anderson, *A Liberal State at War: English Politics and Economics during the Crimean War* (London 1967).
36 Quoted in Dawson, op. cit. p. 123.
37 Hobson, op. cit. p. 90.

and democracy do not go hand in hand; that public opinion is not an infallible specific against war; and that 'the people,' for whatever reason, can be very bellicose indeed. Cobden found himself increasingly isolated, even from the classes which had brought him to power and whose interest in peace he and his followers had taken so much for granted. Nor did they come to their senses when the war was over: 'Sometimes,' Cobden said sadly in 1864, the last year of his life, 'when observing the spirit which pervades so large a part of even our mercantile and manufacturing classes—a spirit of arrogant pride and self-sufficiency—I am almost inclined to resign myself with cynical complacency to some national disaster or check as the only possible cure for our national vices.'[38]

By the end of his life, then, Cobden had lost his innocence. He realised that not only the aristocracy and their hangers-on, but entire peoples could be belligerent. Observing the rising tension over Schleswig-Holstein in the autumn of 1863 he saw that what was looming was no mere *Kabinettskrieg*. If war came, he wrote, 'it will be because of the German people are resolved on war, in which case, like all wars of peoples, it will be a bloody struggle'.[39] Like all wars of peoples! But Europe had already within living memory been torn apart by one such 'war of people', and others had been muttering in the background ever since. How did these conflicts fit in to the diagnosis and prescriptions—disarmament, arbitration, non-intervention, free trade—of a 'Peace Movement' drawn very largely from the prosperous middle classes of the Anglo-Saxon countries and those West of the Rhine?

To many Continental liberals, these prescriptions seemed smug, insular, and totally irrelevant to the historic movements of the century. For them the immediate objective was not peace. It was freedom. And for freedom it might be necessary, and would certainly be justifiable, to fight. 'The map of Europe is to redraw!' exclaimed Giuseppe Mazzini in an open letter to Sir James Graham in 1845: 'Europe is tending to recompose itself in great uniform masses, resulting from a spontaneous popular impulse... New nationalities

---

38 Hobson, op. cit. p. 326.
39 Hobson, op. cit. p 326.

prepare everywhere to form... Which statesmen of yours occupies his thoughts with those configurations of the future whose signs are already on the horizon?'[40] Cobden's doctrine of non-intervention, Mazzini condemned as 'abject and cowardly... atheism transplanted into international life, the deification of self-interest'.[41] In the great, inevitable struggle between the forces of liberty and those of oppression, every man of good-will should stand up and be counted.

So the wave of the 'Peace Movement', which by the middle of the century seemed to be gathering such irresistible momentum, was met head on by an equally strong current of bellicose nationalism. There is little indication in the works either of the utilitarian philosophers or of the Quaker pamphleteers that they had even begun to understand the causes which had set the Revolutionary Wars on foot or the consequences they had had for European society. Cynics might explain British participation in these wars in terms of traditional upper-class obsession with martial glory and middle-class greed or colonial markets, but none of this accounted for the passionate zest with which French armies—and armies composed not of obedient professional soldiers but of French people in arms—flung themselves on their neighbours, overturned their constitutions, and followed Bonaparte to Vienna, to Berlin, to Madrid and to Moscow. Nor did it explain the reaction which this gigantic eruption set on foot in Germany, in Italy, in Russia and in Spain. For the first time millions of men discovered that war was terrible but that it was necessary and might be splendid, and found in the concept of their Nation a cause for which they really were prepared to die.

This is not the place to seek to explore the sociological roots of this nationalism or to explain why the destruction of the monarcho-feudal order in France should have released such a torrent of martial energy, canalised and focused by the concept of a nation to which all its citizens owed a total loyalty and for which they had, if called upon, to lay down their lives. For the French the army was the nation, and the nation founded itself in war: war first to liberate itself,

---

40 Joseph Mazzini, *Life and Writings* (London 1890), vol. III, p. 257-8.
41 Quoted in R.J. Vincent, *Non-Intervention and the International Order* (Princeton U. P. 1974), p. 61.

then to liberate others. Initially the French nation had defined itself in opposition to the monarchy which it first shackled, then destroyed. 'The principle of all sovereignty resides essentially in the Nation,' ran the Declaration of the Rights of Man.[42] 'No body or individual may exercise any authority which does not proceed directly from the Nation.' But very quickly the nation came to define itself in relation and opposition to foreigners. In Germany it had never been anything else. Before the Revolution had begun, Herder had been preaching the excellence of diversity and the need for nations to rediscover and re-emphasise their unique *Volksgeist*.[43] After the disaster of Jena in 1860 Fichte urged Germans to find strength in the deep wells of their national culture to enable them to resist the invader, morally as much as physically: and so far from this movement being directed against their own rulers, the German liberals beseeched their dynasties to put themselves at its head. The apotheosis of German liberalism, as of German nationalism, came when the King of Prussia allowed himself to be made Emperor of Germany, at Versailles in January 1871, after a war fought, consciously and willingly, not by any mere alliance of independent states but by a united German nation.

As for freedom of trade promoting peace, the Prussian economist Friedrich List (1789-1846) argued, as many other have since, that 'Under the existing conditions of the world the result of general free trade would not be a universal republic but on the contrary, a universal subjection of the less advanced nations to the supremacy of the predominant manufacturing, commercial, and naval power.' Commercial protection, pointed out List, was 'a natural consequence of the striving of nations for guarantees of their permanency and prosperity or predominant power.' And war itself could be a factor in economic growth; not only by inducing agrarian states to industrialise themselves, but in general by promoting social mobilisation among belligerent peoples. Finally, such wars need not be purely defensive: 'it must not be ignored,' wrote List, 'that the rounding up of

---

42 Quoted in Carlton Hayes, *The Evolution of Modern Nationalism* (New York 1931), p. 35.

43 *Ideen zur Philosophie der Geschichte der Menschheit* (1784). See Hayes, op. cit p. 29, and Elie Kedourie, *Nationalism* (London 160), p. 55.

the national territory must be reckoned among the most important requirements of nations, that striving to attain it is legitimate, that in some cases it is indeed a legitimate cause of war.'[44]

Until they were part of a nation, then, how could men be free? How could they, in Rousseau's phrase, 'each, uniting with all, nevertheless obey only themselves and remain as free as before'?[45]

The path to freedom, argued the nationalists, could lie only through creation, or rather the liberation, of the nations to which men should be brought to realise (if they did not already) that by language and heritage they belonged. So preached Giuseppe Mazzini, who was only the most ardent and literate of the young evangelists of the creed which had spread from France to Italy, to Poland, to the Balkans, and would ultimately circle the world. The statues which he drew up for Young Italy in 1831 (itself the prototype of a young Germany, a young Poland and ultimately a young Europe) were consciously or unconsciously to be the model for revolutionary nationalist organisations from that day to this. Mazzini preached wars of national liberation. Italy was to be liberated by education and insurrection. 'Education must ever be directed to teach by example, word and pen the necessity of insurrection... Insurrection—by means of guerrilla bands—is the true method of warfare for all nations desirous of emancipating themselves from a foreign yoke... It forms the military education of the people and consecrates every foot of the native soil by memory of some warlike deed.'[46] War, insisted Mazzini, was inevitable: 'desperate and determined war that knows no truce, save in victory or the grave.'[47] Twenty years later he was still calling for 'War, in the noble intention of restoring Truth and Justice, and arresting Tyranny in her inhumane career, of rendering the Nations free and happy and causing God to smile upon them benignantly'; and in particular, calling on the British to take part.[48]

---

44 Silberner, op. cit. pp.136 ff.
45 Jean-Jacques Rousseau, *Du Contrat Social*, Book 1, Chapter 6.
46 Mazzini, *Life and Writings*, vol. I, pp. 106 ff.
47 Ibid. p. 121.
48 Quoted in Kenneth N. Waltz, *Man, the State and War* (New York 1959), p. 110.

These appeals, like those of the Greeks in 1821, the Poles in 1831 and 1864, and the Hungarians in1849,[49] were regarded by Cobden and his colleagues in the Peace Movement with embarrassment and impatience. 'Patriotism, or nationality,' said Cobden, of the Poles in 1831, 'is an instinctive virtue, that sometimes burns the brightest in the rudest and least reasoning minds; and its manifestation bears no proportion to the value of possessions defended and the object to be gained.'[50] In 1849 John Stuart Mill observed how, 'in the backward parts of Europe and even... in Germany, the sentiment of nationality so far outweighs the love of liberty that the people are willing to abet their rulers in crushing the liberty and independence of any people not of their race and language', while a year later the economist Nassau Senior spoke of 'this barbarous feeling of nationality [which] has become the curse of Europe.'[51] In 1856 Cobden denounced the various nationalist pressure groups in England: 'they have *their* scheme of foreign intervention, the wildest and most anarchical of all, for it sets aside the allegiance to treaties and international obligations and would set up a universal propaganda of insurrection and rebellion.'[52] While in 1864 his friend and colleague Henry Richard, who devoted his life to the running of the British Peace Society, declared that 'this idea of nationality is a poor, low, selfish, unchristian idea, at variance with the very principle of an advanced civilisation.'[53]

Richard and his colleagues understandably looked with little pleasure on the foundation, in Paris in 1867, of a *Ligue Internatinale de la Paix et de la Liberté*, which, in contrast to their own more sedate and traditional organisation, regarded the satisfaction of revolutionary and nationalist aspirations as the essential pre-requisite for the

---

49 e.g. Kossuth: 'Should the Czar once more threaten the oppressed humanity, violate the sovereign rights of nations and their independence... humanity expects that Britannia will shake her mighty trident and shout a mighty STOP!' A.J.P Taylor, op. cit. p. 599.

50 Hobson, op. cit. p. 33.

51 L.B. Namier, '1848: The Revolution of the Intellectuals' in *Proceeding of the British Academy, XXX* (London 1944).

52 Hobson, op. cit. p. 177.

53 Beales, op. cit. p. 111.

establishment of a lasting peace. At the first meeting Garibaldi was the guest of honour, and the League laid down, as 'the bases of a permanent peace', the need everywhere to substitute democracy for monarchy, to separate Church from State, and to proceed to the creation, on republican lines, of a United States of Europe;[54] and which recognised that these objectives might have to be achieved by war. Only then would Mazzini's vision be realised, of a Universal Republic of free nations, each adding a distinctive voice to the universal harmony, working out their destinies in peaceful co-operation. The objective of the liberal visionaries remained the same—perpetual and universal peace; but there seemed to be, on the continent of Europe at least, a growing belief that this could be brought about only through further just and necessary wars.

---

54 Ibid. p. 120.

3
THE COMING OF THE FIRST WORLD WAR 1870-1914

The middle decades of the nineteenth century saw the return of large-scale warfare to Europe after forty years of peace. In 1859 France defeated Austria and liberated Italy. In 1864 Prussia and Austria defeated Denmark and 'liberated' Schleswig-Holstein. In 1866 Prussia defeated Austria and created the North German Confederation. And in 1870-1 Prussia and her allies defeated France and established the Second German Reich. From 1859 until 1871 the armies of the European powers were poised to fight campaigns which were, when they came, brief, violent and decisive. At the same time, beyond the Atlantic, the American supporters of the Peace Movement experienced a gigantic Civil War whose objectives the greater part of them, as of their British colleagues, entirely supported. Yet there was little sense that the Peace Movement had been set back by any of these events, or that there was any need to re-examine the propositions on which it was based. Though it would have been difficult for anyone in the Peace Movement to say so explicitly, these great wars had, if anything, helped their cause. The American Republic was at last united under the leadership of the industrial classes, from whom, on the whole, the leaders of that movement came. Two major peoples of Europe, the Germans and the Italians, had come together in nation states, and could now be counted as forces for stability rather than disruption. Certainly there were problems further East, where nationalist aspirations were a growing embarrassment to the rulers of the Russian, the Ottoman and the Habsburg Empires; while few liberals were as yet prepared even to think about the vast, dark, slumbering spaces which lay beyond Europe. But the great nations of Europe and North America could now very plausibly be described as moving onwards and upwards in friendly co-operation towards a stable and permanent peace.

On paper the record for the years 1870 to 1914 looked extremely good. Innumerable functional links were established in the fields of trade, travel and communications, which broadened the common culture of Europe from a thin aristocratic crust deep into the middle classes.[1] Political manifestations of good-will and co-operation abounded. Arbitration, something for which the Peace Movement had worked since its foundation, achieved a spectacular victory with the Alabama award in 1872, made against Britain by a court whose members were selected by the United Kingdom, the United States, Italy, Switzerland and Brazil. Thereafter 194 treaties containing provision for arbitration were signed before 1914, and arbitration procedures were successfully employed in 90 cases. By 1900, according to one historian of the Peace Movement, there were 425 Peace Organisations in being throughout the world, though their distribution was revealing: 46 in Britain, 72 in Germany 16 in France, 15 in the United States, 1 in Russia, and no less than 211 in Scandinavia.[2] Universal Peace Congresses were held annually from 1892. An International Parliamentary Conference was established in 1889 and became institutionalised as the Inter-Parliamentary Union; while of the Hague Conferences held in 1899 and 1907 and of all the hopes attached to them (which were given physical expression in the Palace of Peace, opened in the Hague in 1913 in preparation for a third Hague Conference planned for 1915) it is hardly necessary to speak. The abolition of war, that dream of the eighteenth-century philosophers, seemed almost within reach, and by the means advocated by those philosophers—the civilised intercourse of rational men, representing the aspirations of the broad, peace-loving masses of the world.

---

[1] A good account is to be found in F.S.L. Lyons, *Internationalism in Europe 1815-1914* (Leyden 1963).

[2] Ibid. p. 239.

Yet all this civilised intercourse raised an issue which has plagued liberals from that day to this; what if the people you are dealing with are not, by your standards, civilised? What if their power is based on oppression of nationalities and the denial of human rights? It was all very well for Cobden to advocate 'as little intercourse as possible between the Governments, as much as possible between the nations of the world'; but it is only by intercourse between the governments that issues of war and peace can be settled, that arbitration can be substituted for fighting; and governments are ultimately in a position to determine whether there will be any intercourse between the nations they govern or not. Specifically, then as now, British liberals were divided between those who welcomed the elimination of friction between their own country and the Russian and Ottoman Empires, and those who could barely contain their indignation at seeing the British government shaking the bloody hand of those oppressors of the subject races.

Cobden, until the end of his life, stoutly refused to admit that any problem existed beyond the capacity of 'the hidden hand' to resolve. 'I think there is a Divine Providence which will obviate this difficulty,' he told his critics in the Commons,[3] 'and I don't think that Providence has given it into our hands to execute His behests in this world. I think, when injustice is done, whether in Poland or elsewhere, that the very process of injustice is calculated, if left to itself, to promote its own cure.' But this *laissez-faire* doctrine, in politics as in economics, was decreasingly popular. John Stuart Mill in 1874 expressed his support for armed intervention to redress the balance when a people were fighting for liberty against even a native tyranny, if that tyranny was being helped by foreign arms.[4] An even weightier condemnation came from Gladstone. The view expressed by Cobden and his colleagues, he declared in his Midlothian campaign, 'is not only a respectable, it is even a noble error... but however deplorable wars may be, they are among the necessities of our condition; and there are times when justice, when faith, when the failure of mankind, require

---

3   Dawson, *Richard Cobden & Foreign Policy*, p. 106.
4   J.S. Mill, 'A Few Words on Non-Intervention', *Dissertations and Discussions* (1874) III, p. 256.

a man not to shrink from the responsibility of undertaking them.'[5] The British people, Gladstone maintained, had moral obligations to the subject races of Eastern Europe arising out of the brotherhood of man. On these grounds, not only did he denounce in 1876 the Turkish record in Bulgaria as the 'basest and blackest outrage upon record within the present century, if not within the memory of man,' but he demanded that the British Government should 'apply all its vigour to concur with the other States of Europe in obtaining the extinction of the Turkish executive power in Bulgaria.'[6]

The contrast between Gladstone's attitude as a member of the government in 1854, which went to war to defend the integrity of the Ottoman Empire, and that twenty years later, when, as leader of the opposition, he mounted the Midlothian campaign against the Conservative administration for attempting precisely the same thing, is not to be explained by simple political opportunism. A man of masterful intellect, Gladstone recognised as fully as did his Conservative opponents the need for the maintenance of a balance of political power, or as he himself put it, 'the necessity for regulating the distribution of power in Europe.' 'The absorption of power by one of the great potentates of Europe which would follow the fall of the Ottoman Empire,' he told a Manchester audience in 1853, 'would be dangerous to the peace of the world, and it is the duty of England, at whatever cost, to set itself against such a result.'[7] But as a man of equally strong emotions, he regarded as intolerable the methods employed by tyrannical governments; whether it was the Bourbons of Naples—'the negation of God erected into a system of government'—or the Zaptiehs and Muders, the Bimbashis and Yuzbashis, the Kaimakams and the Pashas of the Unspeakable Turk.[8] Gladstone saw no contradiction in these attitudes. In the white heat of that powerful mind, the two became fused into a single synthesis—the concept of 'the public law of Europe', against which Russian aggression and Turkish atrocities were equally an offence.

---

5   A.J.P. Taylor, op. cit., p. 71.
6   Morley, *Gladstone* II, p. 121.
7   Morley, op. cit. I, p. 359.
8   Ibid. I, p. 290. II, p. 121.

The trouble was of course that no court existed to declare that law or to apply it. The nearest approximation to such a court, in Gladstone's view, was the Concert of European powers, deliberating and acting in unison.[9] But if for any reason they did not so deliberate and act, then the British Government, Gladstone affirmed, had the duty to act on their behalf. In 1882 he explained his conduct in authorising the bombardment of Alexandria by the British fleet and the subsequent occupation of Egypt on these grounds:

> We should not fully discharge our duty if we did not endeavour to convert the present interior state of Egypt from anarchy and conflict to peace and order. We shall look during the time that remains to us to the co-operation of the Powers of civilised Europe. But if every chance of obtaining co-operation is exhausted, the work will be undertaken by the single power of England.

To a protesting John Bright Gladstone explained that he

> [h]ad laboured to the uttermost... to secure that if force were employed against the violence of the Arabs, it should be force armed with the highest sanction of law; that it should be force authorised and restrained by the united Powers of Europe, who in such a case represent the civilised world.[10]

Bright, understandably, was not satisfied with his explanation and resigned from the Cabinet. 'Be the Government Liberal or Tory much the same thing happens', he protested; 'war, with all its horrors and miseries and crimes and cost.'[11]

Very much the same arguments were to be advanced by another British Government seventy-four years later, when in 1956 the Eden Administration attempted in its turn to use military force against Egypt and explained that it was doing so to uphold its conception of the rule of law. Both actions were widely regarded as aggression in the pursuit of self-interest under the cloak of hypocrisy—as is always likely to be the case when a party makes a unilateral statement of its interpretation of the legal position and proceeds to enforce it. But Gladstone's view that simple self-interest did not of itself jus-

---

9   See the chapter on 'Gladstone's European sense' in J.L. Hammond, *Gladstone and the Irish Nation* (London 1938), p. 54.
10 Morley, op. cit. II, p, 241.
11 Trevelyan, *Bright*, p. 437.

tify recourse to war, that war needed to be justified by reference to a common interest of mankind over and above the maintenance of the security state or the maintenance of a stable balance of power, represented a significant development in liberal thinking abut the morality of war.[12] It was a view which recognised the existence of an international community, even if no institutions yet existed to embody it. It recognised the existence of an international morality, even if there were no courts to codify and declare it. While accepting the eighteenth-century ideal of powers working in co-operative balance, it applied moral criteria to the activities of those powers with respect both to their domestic and their international actions. And it recognised that if those criteria were to have any validity, if the public law of Europe was to be more than a phrase, nations might in the last resort have to go to war. This Gladstonian concept of international relations was to be of major significance in shaping the institutions, the perceptions, and the activities of liberal European and American statesmen in the twentieth century.

So by the end of the nineteenth century the passive liberalism of Cobden was as much on the wane in international relations as it was domestic affairs. As one leader of the new generation of liberals, H.N. Brailsford, was to put it, non-interventionism was 'a sterile and impractical deal' which failed to appreciate how far 'the sympathies of our common humanity went beyond the Channel.'[13] Another writer of the new generation, J.A. Hobson, explained that among democratic states the old constraints need no longer apply:

'So long as the conduct and determination of foreign policy remain in the hands of an aristocratic caste or a conspiracy of business interests or a union of the two, the medieval [sic] spirit of jealous statecraft will coalesce with modern business greed to keep alive and stimulate the combative separatist spirit in international relations. But so far as the needs and interests of the peoples can find expression in foreign relations, the deep underlying identity

---

12 See Carsten Holbraad, *The Concert of Europe: a Study in German and British International Theory 1825–1924* (London 1976), esp. pp. 144-8, 165-71.

13 F.M. Leventhal, 'H.N. Brailsford & the Search for a new International Order' in A.J.A. Morris, ed. *Edwardian Radicalism* (London 1974), p. 203.

of human interests will constantly react in efforts to mould international institutions that are favourable to co-operation.'[14]

Here we have Tom Paine again. Adam Smith's 'hidden hand' only needed to be set free from the artificial constraints imposed on it by the self-interest of the ruling classes to go on with its beneficent work.

To this doctrine, the philosopher T.H. Green gave perhaps the most magisterial exposition in the Lectures on the *Principles of Political Obligation* which he delivered at Oxford in the 1870s.

There is no such thing [declared Green] as an inevitable conflict between states... The more perfectly each one of them attains its proper object of giving free scope to the capacities of all persons living on a certain range of territory, the easier it is for others to do so; and in proportion as they all do so the danger of conflict disappears. On the other hand, the imperfect realisation of civil equality, in the full sense of the term, in certain states is in greater or less degree a source of danger to all. The presence in states either of a prerogatived class or of a body of people who... thwarted in the free development of their capacities... always breeds an imagination of there being some competition of interest between states. The privileged class involuntarily believes and spreads the belief that the interest of the state lies in some extension without, not in an improvement of organisation within. A suffering class attracts sympathy from without and invites interference with the state that contains it... *The source of war between states lies in their incomplete fulfilment of their function; in the fact that there is some defect in the maintenance or reconciliation of rights among their subjects.* [My italics][15]

But the right of small nations to struggle for independence, and the problem of weighing the justice of their cause against the requirements of world peace, was to prove a continual source of trouble to liberal thinkers. There were of course those who discounted small nations altogether in the interests of social efficiency and the advance of civilisation—an attitude common in the Fabian movement. 'The State which obstructs international civilisation will have to go,' observed Mr George Bernard Shaw, 'be it big or little. That which advances it should be defended by all the Western powers.'[16] But this

---

14 Hobson, Cobden, p. 408.
15 T.H. Green, *Principles of Political Obligation* (London, reprinted 1922), pp. 170-2.
16 Quoted in K.E. Miller, *Socialism and Foreign Policy* (The Hague 1967), p. 24.

was a minority view. The rights of small nations and of oppressed nationalities had become, by the beginning of the twentieth century a matter, of urgent concern to the intellectuals of the Liberal Party. 'A great part of the inspiration of Liberalism,' wrote one of them, L.T. Hobhouse, in 1904, '... has been drawn from struggles of the nations against Napoleon, of the Eastern Christians against Turkey, of the Poles against Russia, of the Italians against Austria, of the Irish against England.' In his view this was entirely as it should be: 'The safeguards of liberty,' he went on, 'cannot be maintained when one class or one nationality is being held in bondage by another, even though that other holds power nominally in virtue of a majority of votes.'[17]

So as one nationality after another began to assert its identity throughout the world, groups of British sympathisers formed to agitate on their behalf as they had for Kossuth and Mazzini. Armenians and Persians, Boers and Indians, Macedonians, Montenegrins and Bulgarians, Czechs and Croats, Serbs and Ruthenians—why should they not fight for the same liberties as Garibaldi had won for the Italians? H.N. Brailsford began his career fighting for the cause of the Greeks against Turkey in 1897, alongside Italian volunteers who wore the red shirts of Garibaldi.[18] When the Balkan League was formed to fight the Turks in 1912, it enjoyed almost unanimous Liberal support. David Lloyd George welcomed that war as 'enlarging the boundaries of freedom'.[19] Brailsford suggested that the Balkan peoples 'would incur a worse blood-guilt by tolerating oppression' than by appealing to arms, while Norman Angell, fresh from exposing the great illusion that nations might have anything to gain by going to war, qualified his teaching by stating that 'Peace under the Turks was equivalent to war; the liberation of the Balkans was the corridor to civilisation.'[20] The disillusion of 1913 when the victorious Balkan League, instead of peacefully co-operating as liberated

---

17 L.T. Hobhouse, *Democracy and Reaction* (London 1904), pp. 157, 165.
18 H.N. Brailsford, *The War of Steel and Gold* (London 1914), p. 174.
19 A.J.A Morris, *Radicalism against War 1906-1914* (London 1972), p. 352.
20 H. Weinroth, 'Radicalism and Nationalism' in Morris, *Edwardian Radicalism*, pp. 226 ff.

peoples might be expected to do, began immediately to fight one another, was swiftly overtaken by the even greater catastrophe of the Great War. Liberal publicists thereafter were more cautious in their advocacy of unrestricted national self-determination.

This almost unconscious acceptance of the medieval concept of the just war, at least where emerging nationalities were concerned, did not interrupt liberal denunciations of the war-preparations of the Great Powers themselves, for which the arguments of the eighteenth-century rationalists continued to provide ammunition. The conflicts of the Powers, as opposed to those of the emergent nationalities, were still considered to be rooted in the determination of ruling classes concerned to maintain their prestige and their political ascendancy and to increase their financial profits. But during the later part of the nineteenth century those arguments became significantly modified.

It had, as we have seen, been almost common ground among the economists of the earlier part of the nineteenth century that the increasing power and influence of the middle and lower classes, of what Saint-Simon and his followers called *les industrieux*, would, by replacing the vested interests of the aristocracy, almost automatically bring about a more peaceful condition of international relations. Up to a point their expectations were justified. After the upheavals of the mid-century the Great Powers remained at peace for a further forty years during which, as we have seen, the transnational flows of commerce, communications and capital created an increasingly integrated European society. But it was a society in which, in spite of the Peace Movement, the warrior ethic survived and flourished. The peaceful internationalism of Cobden gave way to the protectionism of Joseph Chamberlain and the imperialism of Alfred Milner. In England public schools were established to instil into the children of the middle classes the virtues of discipline, service and patriotism.[21] In Germany, the bourgeoisie of the National Liberal Party loyally supported the 'forward' policies of the Imperial Government and considered it the highest conceivable privilege to hold a reserve

---

21 See e.g. Geoffrey Best, 'Militarism and the Victorian Public School' in Brian Simon and Ian Bradley, eds., *The Victorian Public School* (London 1975) and Rupert Wilkinson, *The Prefects* (1964).

commission in the Imperial Army. In France, Jacobin middle-class traditions of radical militarism provided a far more fruitful soil than did any relics of pre-revolutionary aristocratic martial zest for the nationalist bellicosity to which such figures as Paul Déroulède and general Boulanger gave occasional outlet, but whose full depth was to be revealed only by the Dreyfus Affair. At the dawn of the twentieth century Europe was a very bellicose, very militarist society, and the inflated spirit of patriotism and xenophobia which fuelled an alarmingly intensive arms race could not be laid at the door of the old aristocracy. It was no less virulent among those 'industrious' classes which Saint-Simon and his successors had expected to propagate the spirit of peace.

Why this should have been so remains a historical problem to which there is probably no single, simple solution. We are only just beginning to acquire the intellectual tools to explore and explain the creation of tensions and the movement of opinion in mass societies. Very few historians now, Marxist or non-Marxist, would be satisfied with the simple explanations in terms of economic determinism which were already widespread at the turn of the century and which had become almost orthodox by the inter-war years. The view that 'the bourgeoisie' as such (if it is even legitimate to use such an imprecise term) had an economic interest in international rivalry and war is hardly tenable. There were networks of firms, as Fritz Fischer has shown us in Germany,[22] which profited from armament and imperial expansion, but there were others no less influential whose prosperity depended on the maintenance of the international framework of capitalist intercourse. The rivalry which brought British and German firms into competition overseas was inconsiderable in comparison with the common interest the two countries enjoyed in mutual trade; and in that overseas rivalry business firms were as often the instruments of governments as they were their manipulators.[23] Under critical examination, the part played during this period by the great

---

[22] Fritz Fischer, *Germany's Aims in the First World War* (London 1967) and *War of Illusions* (London 1975).

[23] Eugene Staley, *War and the Private Investor* (New York 1967).

armaments firms in influencing government politics appears decreasingly significant.[24]

It is worth considering, indeed, how far the belligerence of the middle classes during that period was due to a quest for *status* rather than for profit: a desire to make themselves acceptable in societies where a warrior ethic was still dominant; to show that the scions of the counting house and the factory owed nothing to those of the landed gentry when it came to a masculine aggressiveness, martial valour and dedication to the national cause. Historians and political scientists who try to explain the First World War simply in terms of the accumulation of capitalist rivalries and capitalist search for markets are like the drunk in the story who, when asked why he was searching for his lost watch under a street lamp rather than further up the road where he had dropped it, explained that it was because there was more light there.

For Karl Marx and his followers there was no problem. For them the pacific protestations of the Manchester School had been merely a device by which the capitalists had sought to establish their ascendancy and erode that of the aristocracy. Once established, they would fight to preserve that ascendancy against the workers and against one another. The bourgeoisie therefore simply replaced the aristocracy as the ruling class with a vested interest in war, and their overthrow would in turn be necessary before the peoples of the world could live together in peace. For them capitalism, no less than feudalism, inevitably meant war.[25] The Socialist creed thus differed little in essentials from that of Tom Paine, and by the end of the nineteenth century radical liberals and socialists were virtually united in their analysis of the situation. They differed only as to whether peaceful political action would remedy it before it was too late, or whether the disease would yield only to the surgery of violent revolution.

Both groups found equally persuasive the famous thesis of J.A. Hobson, if only because it explained the phenomenon that whereas

---

24 See particularly Clive Trebilcock, 'The British Armaments Industry 1890-1914: False Legend and True Utility' in G. Best and A. Wheatcroft, eds., *War, Economy & the Military Mind* (London 1976).

25 Silberner, op. cit. pp. 267 ff.

inside Europe capitalists seemed to be co-operating amiably enough, in the extra-European world their competition seemed to be provoking dangerous consequences. Published in 1902, immediately after the war in South Africa, Hobson's *Imperialism* boldly explained the complex phenomenon of imperial expansion in terms of its 'economic tap root'. As one nation after another entered the machine economy and adopted advanced industrial methods, he explained,[26] it became more difficult for its manufacturers, merchants and financiers to dispose profitably of their economic resources, and they were tempted more and more to use their governments in order to secure for their particular use some distant underdeveloped country by annexation and protection. It had been in response to these pressures that European governments had been driven to exploit the undeveloped world and been brought repeatedly to the edge of war as a result.

We hardly need to trace the fate of this thesis; how on the one hand it has been buffeted by the work of such historians as Schumpeter, Fieldhouse, Robinson and Gallagher,[27] and on the other apotheosised by Lenin, to become one of the fundamental tenets of contemporary Marxist-Leninism. For our purposes it is enough to point out that, in the era of the Fashoda affair, of the Boxer Rebellion, of the Boer War, and of the two great crises over Morocco in 1905 and 1911, it appeared remarkably persuasive. By 1913 liberals, radicals and socialists had identified imperialism as one of the two great threats to peace.

The other threat was the arms race, for the causes of which they looked no further than the greed and influence of the 'merchants of death'. The armaments firms were denounced in lurid terms:

Too much insistence [wrote one typical Radical organ in 1913][28] cannot be made upon the helpless condition of European civilisation in face of the war spectre whose errors and alarms are, as all the world knows, manipulated and stage-managed by Krupp and their congeners in every land... An un-

---

26 J.A. Hobson, *Imperialism* (London 1902), p. 76.
27 Joseph A. Schumpeter, *Imperialism and Social Classes* (Oxford 1951). D.K. Fieldhouse, *Economics and Empire 1830-1914* (London 1973). R.E. Robinson and J. Gallagher, *Africa and the Victorians* (London 1961).
28 Concord, June 1913, quoted in A.J.A. Morris, *Radicals against War*, p. 335.

scrupulous and inscrutable power of evil, richer than fabled Croesus, panoplied in steel and capable of transmuting the generous blood of heroes into the sordid gold of the safe and snug *actionnaires*, had sprung up in the heart of the nations...

The mouthpiece of the Labour Party, *Labour Leader*, declared at the same time:

> The Armaments Trust is the most terrible of all Capitalism's evils. It is an international conspiracy trading in death... Is it not time that the workers of [all] nations slayed the hideous octopus which lives on their blood?[29]

Here again we can see an understandable confusion of cause and effect. It was hard to see who profited from the frenetic build-up of armaments in Europe during the pre-war years except Krupp and Vickers and Schneider-Creusot and Skoda; and it was easy to isolate these elements in a complex and dangerous situation and identify them as its fundamental causes. It was a view which was to receive the measured support of no less a figure than Sir Edward Grey, a man who in other respects had little time for the radicals:

> Great armaments [he was to write, in a much-quoted passage] lead inevitably to war. The increase of armaments... produces a consciousness of the strength of other nations and a sense of fear. Fear begets suspicion and distrust and evil imaginings of all sorts, till each Government feels it would be criminal and a betrayal of is country not to take every precaution, while every Government regards the precautions of every other Government as evidence of hostile intent.[30]

Was there any answer to this witches' brew which imperialists, finance-capitalists, militarists and armaments-manufactures were cooking up for mankind? There were still those who put their faith in increased information, increased publicity, increased transnational links between peoples: 'We have to aim at a healthier and sounder condition of the body politic,' declared the socialist Alfred Fried in 1908, 'it is the fresh air of open speech, the sunshine of civilisation and of true human fellowship that will destroy the germs that spur us on to international jealousies and internecine strife.'[31] E.D. Morel,

---

29 Quoted in Miller, *Socialism & Foreign Policy*, p. 47.
30 Grey of Falloden, *Twenty-Five Years* (London 1926), vol. I, p. 91.
31 Quoted in Morris, *Radicals against War*, p. 200.

writing in 1912, identified 'secret diplomacy' as the basic cause of international tension and urged that people should be educated in the facts of international life: 'The citizen of education and intelligence... is quite well able to arrive at sound conclusions if the facts are placed before him.'[32] And Brailsford in 1914[33] saw the problem as being 'how the will of a democracy, how the small governing class, which everywhere promotes its own economic ends and imposes them on public opinion, *as it becomes enlightened*, [my italics] may check and guide the working of diplomacy.'

Most English liberals, when they spoke of 'educated public opinion', clearly had in mind people of the same stamp as themselves, the middle-class heirs of the enlightenment, and those industrious, educated mechanics whom they could recruit into their ranks. Their socialist colleagues, especially those on the Continent, cast their net wider. By 'the people' they meant the proletariat: the wage-slaves who, they declared, were always the losers even from a successful war. Brailsford himself had come to this conclusion, as Charles Trevelyan was soon to do in his turn. The liberals, wrote Brailsford scathingly,

> Talking today of disarmament and arbitration... will work tomorrow for a party which is hardly less dependent than its rival on the great contractors and bankers who maintain the modern connection of diplomacy and finance. The work of education and organisation on behalf of peace is carried on adequately only by the Socialist parties, and they alone represent a force whose undivided vote will always be cast against militarism and imperialism.[34]

Such of course was the doctrine of the leaders of the Socialist International. 'Do you know what the proletariat is?' Jean Jaurès

---

32 Quoted in L.W. Martin, *Peace without Victory* (Yale U.P. 1958), p. 11.

33 H.N. Brailsford, *The War of Steel and Gold* (London 1914), p. 170.

34 Ibid. p. 161. It was no new thing for the middle-class liberals, disillusioned with their own sector of society, to look to the workers to redeem the time. Cobden, finding the people of Lancashire 'growing conservative and aristocratic with their prosperous trade' felt it necessary for the Peace Movement to look to the common people. 'After all, our business must be with the masses—keep them right and we can't go wrong.' [W.H. Dawson, *Cobden & Foreign Policy*, p.143.] Bright in 1878 had declared, 'If the Trade Unions would speak out for peace, there would be no war. There are men and classes to whom it is sometimes gain; to the working man it is only loss.' [Beales, *History of Peace*, p. 157.]

demanded of a rally in Brussels on the eve of the war; 'Masses of men who collectively love peace and abhor war!'[35] At the meeting of the International at Basel in November 1912 the proletariat was declared to be 'the herald of world peace'. The crisis provoked by the First Balkan War enabled the Socialist parties of Europe to organise a series of impressive mass demonstrations in favour of peace, including one in Berlin on 20 October allegedly attended by over 250,000 people—which lent some credibility to the warnings issued from Basel that the proletariat would not permit themselves to be dragged into war. 'The International is strong enough to speak in this tone of command to those in power and if necessary follow up their words with deeds. War on war, peace for the world, hurrah for the worker's international!'[36]

Nevertheless the proposal, put forward by the Frenchman Gustav Hervé, that the workers should protest against the outbreak of war by an immediate general strike, was not accepted. The proletariat may have been international, but it was not supra-national. In liberal thought the strands of nationalism and internationalism were still intertwined. Jaurés wrote in 1911:

> Those Frenchmen, if there are any left, who say it is all the same to them whether they live under German troopers or French troopers... commit a sophism which by its very absurdity makes refutation difficult. The truth is that wherever there are countries, that is historical groups having a consciousness of their continuity and their unity, any attack on the freedom and integrity of those countries is an attack against civilisation, a relapse into barbarism.[37]

For the German socialists, Bebel had said much the same;

> The soil of Germany, the German fatherland, belongs to us the German masses as much and more than to the others. If Russia, the champion of terror and barbarism, went to attack Germany to break and destroy it... we are as much concerned as those who stand at the head of Germany.[38]

And the Englishman Brailsford agreed:

---

35 George Haupt, *Socialism and the Great War* (Oxford U.P. 1972), p. 11.
36 James Joll, *The Second International* (London 1955), p. 153.
37 Ibid., p. 112.
38 Loc. cit.

The right of every nationality to defend its liberty and its identity against conquest is a right which Socialism has always been the first to respect and will be the last to abandon. The general adoption of Hervé's theories by the more advanced nations would be merely an invitation to the less advanced to conquer and enslave them... The country which had the most socialists would be the first to be devoured and exploited by its neighbours.[39]

The working classes, then, were depicted by their leaders as being no less patriotic than any other section of the community. Was there any reason to suppose that they were in practice more passionately attached to the cause of peace? We have seen how disillusioned Cobden had become as a result of the Crimean War. During the Boer war his successors had fared no better. Objectors to the war were vilified in the popular press, had their meetings broken up, were subjected to physical attack. After that experience L.T. Hobhouse confessed that he could no longer believe that, since wars resulted from selfish class interest, democracies would necessarily be peace-loving: 'One nation may act as selfishly, callously and cruelly in relation to another as one class in relation to another,' he wrote. 'In the doctrine that the people as a whole can have no sinister interests, foreign and colonial relations are left out of account.'[40] In Germany, Max Weber came to the same conclusion: 'One cannot see why strong state socialist communities should disdain to squeeze tribute out of the weaker communities for their own partners where they could do so,' he wrote, 'just as happened everywhere in early history.' As to the 'pacific interests' of the masses, he was deeply sceptical. They were, in his view, more easily swayed by emotional influences than were their rulers; they had in fact, in spite of what the Socialists said, *less* to lose from war than had the possessing classes. War could be seen as opening for them tantalising opportunities of social change and advancement.[41] And George Bernard Shaw expressed his idiosyncratic view of the situation: 'All classes, in proportion to their lack of travel and familiarity with foreign literature, are bellicose, prejudiced against foreigners,

---

39 Brailsford, op. cit. p. 185.
40 L.T. Hobhouse, *Democracy and Reaction* (London 1904), p. 141.
41 H. Gerth and C. Wright Mills, ed., *From Max Weber, Essays in Sociology* (London 1947), pp. 169, 171.

fond of fighting as a cruel sport—in short, dog-like in their notions of foreign policy.'[42]

The outbreak of the First World War was to confirm all these fears. The peacemaking leaders of the International found themselves isolated and unpopular in their own countries. Victor Adler, the Austrian socialist, observing the enthusiasm with which the Viennese crowds welcomed the prospect of war with Serbia, sadly concluded, 'it is better to be wrong with the working classes than right against them.'[43] The German Social Democrat Wilhelm Dittman justified his party's vote in support of war credits in the Reichstag on the grounds, 'the Party could not act otherwise. It would rouse a storm of indignation among men at the front and people at home against the Social Democratic party if it did. The Socialist organisation would be swept clean away by popular resentment.'[44] The pacifist Ramsay MacDonald, after a brave protest in the House of Commons, had to abdicate the leadership of his party. Working-class reactions in 1914, at least in Western Europe, made it clear that, rightly or wrongly, the proletariat did not regard this war as being in any sense a remote question of state policy brought about by the machinations of self-interested elites. They saw it as a matter of national survival in which they were as intimately concerned as anyone else.

So convinced were the liberals that if war came it would be as the result of imperialist and capitalist conflicts, that this new War of Nations took them completely by surprise. For by 1914 the feeling was growing among liberal thinkers that the danger of war was receding precisely because these economic rivalries had proved a great deal less dangerous than had been expected. The British and the French had composed their differences in Egypt. The French and the Germans had composed their differences in Morocco. The Germans and the British were co-operating amicably in the Ottoman Empire. The Powers of Europe, by their prompt and successful co-operation over the Balkan crisis of 1912, had revealed both a common will and a capacity to keep the peace—to act in the Gladstonian role as the

---

42 Quoted in Miller, *Socialism & Foreign Policy*, p. 23.
43 Joll, op. cit., p. 153.
44 Ibid. p. 176.

guardians of international public law. And behind all this could be seen the international interests of finance capital, of the great banking houses and the industrial combines, whose fear of war was faithfully reflected in the behaviour of the international stock markets whenever a crisis occurred. Might not Cobden have been right after all? Was not the creation of a closely-knit international network of common financial and commercial interests the best possible guarantee of peace?

Norman Angell, who has been described with some reason as 'the ablest pamphleteer who has used the English language since Thomas Paine',[45] argued that it was. His book *The Great Illusion* did not maintain that war was impossible—only that it was useless; and that 'on a general realisation of this truth depends the solution of the problem of armaments and warfare.'[46] The capitalist, wrote Angell, 'has no country, and he knows... that arms and conquests and juggling with frontiers serve no ends of his and may very well defeat them.'[47] He believed that it was no longer for one nation to seize by force the wealth and trade another. 'If credit and commercial contract are to be tampered with in an attempt at confiscation,' he argued, 'the credit-dependent wealth is undermined, and its collapse involves that of the conqueror; so that if conquest is not to be self-injurious it must respect the enemy's property, in which case it becomes economically futile.'[48] What was needed was to convince everyone of this—not so much to *appeal* to public opinion as to *educate* it. Popular ideas were still dominated by archaic and outmoded concepts inherited from a former era, and 'a change in the political climate of Europe can only come about as the result of a change of thought.'[49]

Brailsford, whose equally influential *War of Steel and Gold* appeared in the summer of 1914, agreed that public opinion must be educated: 'There must be a more educative propaganda, a more conscious effort

---

45 Brailsford, *War of Steel & Gold*, p. 161.
46 Norman, Angell, *The Great Illusion* (London 1913), p. vi. The first edition appeared in 1909.
47 Ibid. p. 309.
48 Ibid. p. viii.
49 Ibid. p. 327.

to fix principles, before any democracy can be trusted to stand firm in moments of national crisis.'[50] And he agreed with Angell, that although there were powerful groups in European society drawing huge profits from armaments and the bloodless struggle for a balance of power, 'Few modern Europeans want a war, and of those, fewer still have the sinister strength to declare it when the moment of decision arrives.'[51] Like Bentham before him, Brailsford believed that if commercial rivalries could be settled, no further cause for war remained. 'In Europe the epoch of conquest is over,' he wrote, 'and save in the Balkans and perhaps on the fringes of the Austrian and Russian Empire, it is as certain as anything in politics that the frontiers of our national states are finally drawn. My own belief is that there will be no more wars among the six Great Powers.'[52]

This unfortunately-timed prophecy might have been taken as evidence of British ignorance and insularity if Continental socialists had not shown themselves equally optimistic. In June 1914 the Second International declared that the international situation was characterised by general détente; and while a few hopeful spirits attributed that to the effect of the impressive popular demonstrations in favour of peace the previous year in overawing the ruling classes, there was broad agreement with the view expressed by Karl Kautsky that, though imperialism certainly created dangerous tensions, 'there are at present in the same society conflicting elements which are economically interested in the preservation of peace and which thus encourage the growth of the other factors.' Kautsky's colleague Bebel pronounced that 'the greatest guarantee for the preservation of the world today is found in the international investments of capitalism.' And in June 1914 the Dutch socialist Vliegen, while admitting the dangers of militarism and of the arms race, wrote, 'there is a complete absence of the real and tangible interests that could justify a war.'[53]

---

50 Brailsford, op. cit. p. 160.
51 Ibid. p. 169.
52 Ibid. p. 35.
53 Haupt, *Socialism and the Great War*, pp. 150-159.

Thus, hypnotised by the apparent transformation of war-mongering capitalists into a strong force for peace, liberals and socialists in 1914 underestimated the true dangers: those arising from the forces inherent in the states-system of the balance of power which they had for so long denounced, and those new forces of militant nationalism which they themselves had done so much to encourage. It was these which combined to destroy the transnational community they had laboured to create, almost beyond hope of repair. Yet overwhelmingly, when they went to war in 1914, liberals everywhere did so with a clear conscience. They were fighting for irreproachable causes: to assert or to defend national rights; to defend their native soil against invasion; or, in the case of the British, to uphold the Gladstonian concept of the public law in Europe.

4
ARMS AND THE COVENANT 1914–1935

At the end of the last chapter we saw how it came about that to most European liberals, even to those who had been most active in the Peace Movement, the First World War appeared at its outset to be a profoundly just war in which they could partake with a good conscience. In Russia they believed that they were fighting for the self-determination of the Slav peoples. In Germany and Austria they fought to protecct Europe from Russian despotism. In France, Belgium and Serbia they were certainly fighting wars of national self-defence. Italians fought to complete the liberation of their people from Austrian rule. And British liberals believed themselves to be upholding the public law of Europe and the rights of small nations against brutal and unprovoked aggression.

Yet most British liberals knew that it was not so easy as that. The German invasion of Belgium was certainly a clear breach of international law which by any conventional standard of political morality provided a sufficient cause for intervention. But it was clear that even if Germany had not invaded Belgium, Britain could not have remained neutral in the conflict for very long, whether she had any secret obligations to France or not. Edward Grey explained the position to the House of Commons in terms they could all understand and from which it was difficult for them to dissent:

If, in a crisis like this, we run away from those obligations of honour and interest as regards the Belgian Treaty, I doubt whether, whatever material force we might have at the end, it would be of very much value in the face of the respect we should have lost. And I do not believe, whether a great Power stands outside this war or not, it is going to be in a position at the end of it to exert its superior strength... to prevent the whole of the West of Europe opposite to us—if that had been the result of the war—falling under the domination of a single Power.[1]

So underlying the issue of the public law of Europe there lay the harsh calculations of that 'foul idol', the balance of power. But underlying those again was an ideological element which was to increase in strength as the war went on and became the dominant theme in liberal justifications of war in the twentieth century. Germany had to be fought not simply to punish a breach of international law, or to maintain a continental balance. She had to be fought because she was in the grip of a militaristic and destructive philosophy which had to be destroyed if the world was to be made 'safe for democracy'.

It took only a very few days for British liberal opinion to come to this conclusion. On 31 July 1914 the *Manchester Guardian* was still crying a plague on both the belligerent houses and voicing its fear 'lest by some hidden contract England has been technically committed behind her back to the ruinous madness of a share in the wicked gamble of a war between two militaristic leagues on the Continent.' A week later, (6 August) another liberal organ, the *Daily News*, reluctantly accepted a *fait accompli*: 'It would have been just and prudent and statesman-like for England to have remained neutral... [but] a mistaken course of policy, pursued over ten years, has led us to the terrible conflict in which we are now engaged... [and] being in...we must win.' Two days later it expressed the hope that 'barbarism... is fighting its last battle.' At the end of September it printed an editorial by the great liberal journalist A.G. Gardiner to the effect that Britain now stood for 'the spirit of light against the spirit of darkness.'[2] About the same time H.G. Wells coined the phrase 'the war to end war'. By November, when the German armies were exerting the last reserves of their strength to break through the British lines in the First Battle of Ypres, most liberals would probably have endorsed G.M. Trevelyan's view that 'this war is life or death'.[3]

---

1 Grey of Falloden, *Twenty-Five Years* (London 1925), vol. II, p. 306.
2 All quotations from L.W. Martin, *Peace Without Victory* (Yale University Press 1958), pp. 46-50.
3 See above, p. 11.

Most, but not all. Charles Trevelyan, as we have seen, was among those who resigned from the government rather than condone British participation in the war. Ramsay MacDonald maintained the opposition to which he had given solitary voice in the Commons. Together with the two prolific publicists Norman Angell and E.D. Morel, with MacDonald's colleague in the Labour Party, Philip Snowden, and one other upper-class recruit, the former diplomat Arthur Ponsonby, these men met within a few days of the outbreak of war to set up the Union for Democratic Control. It was not their object to oppose the war: a German victory was not likely to advance the cause they had at heart. It was to preserve clarity of thought about a foreign policy while the war was being fought, and to work towards the emergence after the war of an international system more in accordance with their ideals; to ensure, in fact, that this would really be a war to end wars.

The views of the Union for Democratic Control were set out in a pamphlet by its most active member, E.D. Morel, *The Morrow of the War*. This expounded the orthodox liberal doctrine about the causation of wars in terms which showed how little British liberal thinking about international politics had changed since the days of Jeremy Bentham and Tom Paine.[4]

The theory of 'the Balance of Power' and secret diplomacy [wrote Morel] are two factors which, in combination, make for war. Two other factors intimately associated with these ensure its certainty. They are: a constant progression in expenditure upon armaments, and the toleration of a private armaments interest.

There should therefore be, as part of the peace settlement, drastic reduction of armaments, and general nationalisation of armaments manufacture. There should be adequate machinery for ensuring democratic control of foreign policy. No improvement could be hoped for on the international scene 'if the political and democratic system and methods which preceded the war are maintained afterwards and if the settlement rests solely in the hand of those committed by as-

---

4   E.D. Morel, *The Morrow of the War* (London 1914). On the UDC see Marvin Swartz, *The Union of Democratic Control in British Politics during the First World War* (Oxford 1971).

sociations and tradition to such a system.' No transfers of territory should take place without the consent of the populations, obtained by internationally-supervised plebiscites. And most important of all:

> The Foreign Policy of Great Britain shall not be aimed at creating Alliances for the purpose of maintaining the Balance of Power, but shall be directed to concerted action between the Powers, and the setting up of an International Council, whose deliberations and decisions shall be public, with such machinery for securing international agreement as shall be the guarantee of abiding peace.

So the idea of a League of Nations, which had been gradually maturing since the Thirty Years War, was put forward, no longer as the speculation of the occasional visionary, but as the firm proposal of a group of active politicians, who were rapidly to gain for it widespread and influential support. In the autumn of 1914 a group was formed, under the chairmanship of the elder statesman Lord Bryce, to study future world organisation, and this developed in March 1915 into the League of Nations Society. The object of this society was the creation, at the end of the war, of a League open to all states of the world, who would pledge themselves to submit all disputes to arbitration and which would if necessary use severe sanctions to compel aggressor states to do so. Shortly afterwards an equally august body came into being in the United States—a 'League to Enforce Peace' under the presidency of the former President William Howard Taft. This did not speak simply of 'sanctions'. Its declared objective was 'a world organisation which will tend to prevent war by forcing its members to use peaceable means first... and to make immediate and certain war upon any nation which goes to war without a previous hearing of the dispute.'[5]

But was such an aspiration realistic, without a transformation in the nature of the governments themselves? Morel himself did not believe so. 'The idea of a federalised Europe,' he wrote, in *The Morrow of the War*,

> regulated by an Areopagus, involving the disappearance, or substantial reduction of standing armies and navies and the submission of all disputes to a Common Council... cannot be attained until the constitutionally-gov-

---

5 Beales, *A History of Peace*, p. 293.

erned democracies of the West are brought to realise how impossible it is that their... well-being can be secured under a system of government which leaves them at the mercy of the intrigues and imbecilities of professional diplomats and of the ambitions of military castes.[6]

The same point was made even more forcefully by the young Bertrand Russell in a pamphlet he wrote for the UDC, *The Foreign Policy of the Entente*:[7]

> The interests of British democracy do not conflict at any point with the interests of mankind. The interests of the British governing classes conflict at many points with the interests of mankind... A policy of adventure and national prestige appeals most forcibly to the rich, while the wage-earning class, *if it understood its own interest and were not caught by the glamour of Jingo phrases*, [my italics] would insist upon a policy of peace and international conciliation.

Here once more we have the liberal credo: peace depended on the spread of democracy—or at least, *guided* democracy. But the logical corollary of that belief was that democracy must be uniformly distributed among the nations of the world. It was that which in the eyes of so many liberals made the fight against German militarism a just war. But this implied an abandonment of the liberal belief in non-intervention, and the acceptance of interventionism of a new and far-reaching kind. It could hardly be said that the Allies were fighting on behalf of the German people against oppressive government. They were fighting to make the German people change their system of government, whether they wanted to or not, in the interests of world peace.

The UDC and its associates did, with great courage and consistency, continue to draw a doubtfully tenable distinction between German militarism and the German people. They assumed that if only the German people knew the facts and could make their wishes felt, all differences between them and their neighbours could be peacefully resolved. It was therefore a firm plank in their platform that Germany should not be humiliated and destroyed, but that after her defeat (and presumably after the advent of a 'democratic' government

---

6 Morel, op. cit.
7 Bertrand Russell, *The Foreign Policy of the Entente* (London 1914).

to power) she should be treated as a full member of the society of nations. It led them to press an embarrassed Government to make declarations of peace aims, whose moderation would make clear to the German people the extent to which they had been misled by their own leaders.[8] At the same time they showed a reserve towards the claims of smaller nation states which was in significant contrast to the enthusiasm some of them had displayed at the time of the First Balkan War. The support for 'Gallant Little Serbia' in the popular press at the beginning of the war, and the later attempts by the Allied governments to stir up racial strife within the Austrian Empire were in themselves enough to make the liberals reconsider some of their own presuppositions. Bernard Shaw was predictably contemptuous of the claims of the small nations: 'I hold no brief for small States as such,' he wrote,[9] 'and most vehemently deny that we are in any way bound to knight errantry on their behalf as against big ones... They multiply frontiers, which are nuisances, and languages, which have made a confusion since the building of Babel.' More surprising was the venom with which the gentle Goldsworthy Lowes Dickinson, writing after the war, was to express himself on the subject. Serbia he described as a 'little primitive, barbarous, aggressive state' and the Balkan States in general as 'those bellicose hordes of primitive and violent men.'[10] Some liberals, Norman Angell among them, began to wonder whether it was not nationalism, rather than capitalism, that was the real enemy of peace, and whether there was any necessary connection between the two. Would National Socialism be any better?[11]

And would the full implementation of the national idea really lead to a more stable Europe? Brailsford was one of those who contemplated the prospect with something like horror. In 1917 he denounced the activities of such active supporters of Central Europe

---

8 Kenneth E. Miller, *Socialism & Foreign Policy* (The Hague 1967), p. 54. Martin, op. cit., p. 66.
9 Miller, op. cit. p. 51.
10 G. Lowes Dickinson, *War: its Nature, Cause & Cure* (London 1923), pp. 66, 69.
11 Norman Angell, *The Unseen Assassins* (London 1932), passim. See below, p. 95.

nationalist movements as R.W. Seton-Watson and L.B. Namier. It had, he wrote, become 'a generous pastime with our scholars to reconstruct the map of Europe on the basis of nationality, and so sure were those idealists that the reign of force would be abolished that few of them even paused to consider whether a little land-locked Bohemia or diminished but independent Hungary could maintain their sovereignty under the pressure of the great military Empires which would surround them.' These new states, he foresaw, 'would be forced, as they have always been, to oscillate between the German and Russian systems.' Worse, with their minorities, 'each of these little States would reproduce in little the hatreds and confusions of Europe.'[12] Ironically, therefore, as Allied war aims hardened in favour of the destruction of the German and Austrian political systems in the name of democracy and of national self-determination, the voice of the liberal opposition was heard defending the preservation of the power of Germany and the structure of the Austrian Empire in order to maintain a viable state-system in Europe; something not far removed indeed from a balance of power. By the end of the war, as Mr A.J.P. Taylor has sardonically pointed out, the UDC and the radicals were urging something very much like a restoration of the *status quo* of 1914.[13]

But by 1917–18 matters were out of the hands of the British liberal dissenters; out of the hands, almost, of the British government. The United States had entered the war on the side of the Allies, virtually guaranteeing victory on her own terms; terms which were, to all appearances, exactly those for which liberals had been fighting ever since Thomas Paine had hailed the new Republic as the embodiment of all those virtues which the old world so conspicuously lacked.

Before 1914 almost the only citizens of the United States who devoted any sustained thinking to the problems of international relations had been those members of peace societies and international congresses who had been in such constant and fruitful contact with their contacts in Europe, playing an increasingly dominant part in these activities as their wealth and numbers increased. Andrew

---

12 H.N. Brailsford, *A League of Nations* (London 1917), pp. 4, 101.
13 Taylor, *The Trouble Makers*, p. 149.

Carnegie had set up his Endowment for International Peace in 1910 with a fund of ten million dollars, to study the cause of war, the development of international law, and the problem of influencing opinion against war; and that sturdy heart has been pumping blood into the veins of peace organisations through the world ever since. The American Peace Society had greeted the outbreak of war in 1914 with the *schadenfreude* of a Cassandra seeing her worst prophecies coming true: 'The wonder is not that the war broke out this summer upon Europe, but that it did not begin years ago...' They did not at this stage see the war as one for the defence of democracy and the public law of Europe against militarism and aggression. 'The real cause of conflict,' they wrote, 'is the piled up armaments and war materials in Europe... No delusion was ever greater than that implements of war... are guarantees of peace and safety.'[14]

This mood of 'a plague on both your houses' harmonised well with the teaching and activities of the Union of Democratic Control, whose leaders found many sympathetic ears in Washington. There was little in the speeches of President Wilson up till April 1917 that had not been foreshadowed in UDC pamphlets—particularly the great speech of 22 January 1917 when, claiming to speak 'for liberals and friends, humanity in every nation and of every programme of liberty,' he demanded 'peace without victory... a peace between equals.' People should no longer be handed about from sovereignty to sovereignty as though they were property. Civil liberties should be assured to national and religious minorities, disarmament be set on foot, and an international organisation created 'wielding such power that no nation could resist it.'[15] All of which was to be expanded a year later into the Fourteen Points which, in Laurence Martin's words, 'constituted the most comprehensive and striking presentation yet of a liberal programme, almost exactly endorsing the aims of the British radicals.'[16]

'Peace without victory', 'peace between equals': this presupposed the kind of civilised discourse between rational men on which

---

14 Beales, op. cit. p. 290.
15 L.W. Martin, *Peace without Victory*, pp. 124-125.
16 Ibid. p. 161.

Bentham had founded his hopes of the international system. But once the United States began fighting the mood changed. Wilson took the Americans into the war in the crusading spirit of the French Revolution, a spirit which Tom Paine would certainly have applauded, the spirit of *guerre aux châteaux, paix aux chaumières*. It was a crusade which the men of the Peace Movement endorsed up to the hilt. 'This war,' declared the American Peace Society, 'is not a war of territory, of trade routes or of commercial concerns, but of eternal principles.' 'There can be no end of war until after the collapse of the existing German imperial government.' The Trustees of the Carnegie Endowment stated in April 1917 that 'the most certain means of instituting a durable peace among the nations is to pursue the War against the Imperial German Government until the final victory of democracy.'[17] And this Wilson promised to do: 'There can be but one issue. The settlement must be final. There can be no compromise. No half-way decision would be tolerable. No half-way is conceivable.'[18]

This view was argued with the characteristic wit and ferocity by the radical social thinker Thorstein Veblen, on the eve of America's entry into the war. Veblen considered that peace would come only when the upper classes, not only of Germany, but also of Britain had been effectively wiped out, since the chances of a successful settlement 'appear to be very largely bound up with the degree of vulgarisation due to overtake the several directorates of the belligerent nations.'[19] Peace could be made only on the basis of 'unconditional surrender of the formidable warlike nations.'[20] Veblen had no belief in the fundamentally democratic nature of German society. The kind of democratic regime which would be indispensable as a working basis for a League of Peace, he considered, 'would from the outset have to be enforced against the most desperate resistance of the ruling

---

17 Beales, op. cit. pp. 291-2.
18 Quoted by Elie Kedourie, *Nationalism* (London 1960), p.130.
19 Thorstein Veblen, *An Inquiry into the Nature of Peace* (New York 1917. 2nd Edn. 1919), pp. 256, 276.
20 Ibid. pp. 239, 243.

classes... backed by the stubborn loyalty of the subject populace.'[21] The German people, in fact, must be forced to be free.

Veblen saw clearly two things which most liberal thinkers preferred to ignore. One was the cultural heterogeneity of the world. Some societies, for good historical reasons, may at times be more bellicose and hierarchical than others, and one has to accept either the risks of peacefully co-existing with them or the responsibilities of cultural imperialism—of their conquest and re-education. The other was that wars conducted by democratic societies are seldom ended by moderate, negotiated peace. When Bentham looked to public opinion as the great instrument of pacification he could never have conceived of the mass passions that war would unchain in industrial societies. It was public opinion in Britain, France and Italy, acting on impeccably democratic politicians, which made impossible a rational peace. Wilson spoke gallantly of his ability to 'reach the peoples of Europe over the heads of their rulers',[22] but he could not reach them half so effectively as could Lloyd George, Clemenceau and Orlando; politicians who, whatever their own feelings, accepted the truth of Victor Adler's dictum that it was better to be wrong with the people than right against them. Wilson was himself tragically to make the same discovery.

So the Versailles settlement was made, and it lay on the liberal conscience like a burden of original sin. 'It was exactly as we had prophesied,' wrote Charles Trevelyan, 'the Imperialist War had ended in the Imperialist Peace.'[23] Behind a façade of high-flown liberal sentiments about democracy and national delf-determination, the British government and its allies had conducted the war as they had conducted all previous wars—for the national self-aggrandisement of their own states, making secret agreements to distribute enemy possessions among themselves, taking no account of the wishes of the peoples concerned. The one clear note which Liberal leaders had struck at the beginning of the war, Trevelyan pointed out,

---

21 Ibid. p. 243.
22 Martin, op. cit. p. 179.
23 Quoted in John F. Naylor, *Labour's International Policy* (London 1969), p.4.

was the right of all peoples to self-determination. They called for sympathy for Croats and Czecho-Slovaks and Italians under Austrian rule. They demanded the independence of Poland. But when Europe began to be repartitioned at Paris and a dozen new oppressions were substituted for the old ones, there was no protest in the name of principle or justice or Liberalism against the fate of Germans annexed to Poland, Austrians to Italy and Czecho-slovakia, Serbs and Hungarians to Romania, Bulgarians to Serbia... Their Liberal 'war to end war' has closed with an imperialist peace to perpetuate national injustice and armaments.[24]

On this Trevelyan spoke for the UDC liberals as a whole, and at the end of the war this group transferred their loyalties *en masse* to the Labour Party: Norman Angell and Arthur Ponsonby, Charles Trevelyan and E.D. Morel, Noel Buxton, Goldsworthy Lowes Dickinson and Leonard Woolf.[25] Their old associates H.N. Brailsford and J.A. Hobson had already preceded them. Henceforward the liberal conscience was to speak primarily, though by no means exclusively, through the organs of the Labour Party. 'The Labour Party,' in Leonard Woolf's words, 'inherited its foreign policy from Cobden and Bright through Gladstone Liberalism.'[26]

Rejection of the injustice of the Versailles *diktat* became one of the earliest and most fundamental principles of Labour, as it was of Liberal foreign policy. It was, declared the Executive of the Independent Labour Party, 'a capitalist, imperialist and militarist imposition. It aggravates every evil which existed before 1914. It does not give the world peace, but the ceratainty of other and more calamitous wars.'[27] Labour critics picked specifically on the injustice of subjecting millions of Germans to alien rule in Czechoslovakia; on the proposed annexation to France of the Saar; on the annexation to Poland of German areas of West Prussia; and on the prohibition, in defiance of the wishes of the population, of any *Anschluss* between Austria and Germany.[28] Sympathy for the Germans was whole-hearted and generous, but there was less affection wasted on the French.

---

24 Charles Trevelyan, *From Liberalism to Labour* (London 1921), p. 43.
25 Miller, *Socialism and Foreign Policy*, p. 83.
26 Quoted by Miller, op. cit., p. 252.
27 Miller, op. cit., p. 93.
28 Loc. cit. Also Taylor, *The Troublemakers*, pp.176-7.

It was difficult indeed to fit French policy towards Germany into any conventional sterotype. The popular support so clearly enjoyed by M. Poincaré in his punitive treatment of the defeated Germans could hardly be explained in terms of capitalism, imperialism, or the machinations of a traditional ruling class. Brailsford concluded that 'in spite of Republican forms, a nation of small peasant-owners and small investors never will be Liberal in the British sense of the word.'[29] That was the trouble: so very few people, outside Britain, Scandinavia and United States, *were* liberal 'in the British sense of the word'.

Could nothing be rescued from the wreck of the Versailles settlement? Certainly: there was the League of Nations, whose Covenant embodied all the aspirations of lovers of peace for the past two hundred years. There were those, Charles Trevelyan among them, who regarded the League as being no more than an alliance of capitalist, imperialist powers to enforce an unjust peace, and who despaired, as E.D. Morel had despaired, of seeing good fruit from so rotten a tree; but most agreed that it was the best that could be expected under the circumstances. 'Democratic control of the Society of Nations,' J.A. Hobson had written during the war, 'as of the several nations, is the only full security for peace and progress, but that is no ground for refusal to support the best beginnings of that international society which under the existing ciscrumstances are attainable.'[30] The general hope of liberal thinkers was that the League would at least provide a basis on which to build a new world order. 'Belief in the League of Nations as a substitute for swollen armaments and rival alliances,' said Ramsay Muir, 'should henceforth be the pivot of British foreign policy.' Gilbert Murray suggested, in the true spirit of Bentham, that 'wars caused, or made more likely, by the mutual prejudices of nations, by their habit of working always apart and in secrecy, [would be] met by the immense field of international co-operation which the League proposes, and its absolute insistence upon frank interchange of information.'[31]

---

29 Miller, op. cit. p. 250.
30 J.A. Hobson, *The Fight for Democracy* (London 1917), p. 54.
31 Miller, op. cit. p. 251.

This became the dominant view. The Labour Party in 1928[32] called for 'whole-hearted support of the League of Nations as the arbiter of international peace and order, in preference to the basing of peace upon separate pacts, ententes and alliances.' But support for the League as the focus for a new style of foreign policy reached far beyond the Labour and Liberal Parties. The League of Nations Union under its Conservative Chairman Viscount Cecil established branches throughout the country and enjoyed all-party support. With some reason it has been described as 'the most successful organisation of its kind since the Anti-Corn Law League,'[33] but unlike that League it expressed a broad consensus of all parties and all classes. It would probably be fair to describe it as representing the mainstream of political opinion in Britain in the early 1930s. It was the chief conduit through which that general reaction against the whole concept of war, which typified the inter-war years, found expression.

One of the many virtues of the League of Nations Movement was that it did not lose itself in pious generalities. The implications of the Covenant were repeatedly spelled out in its literature and its propaganda. Much of it derived from Bentham and his contemporaries: compulsory arbitration, disarmament, and the need for all treaties between States to be publicly registered if they were to be binding in international law. But there was, in addition, a new realisation that peace should not imply an uncritical acceptance of the status quo; that the League had to take account of the obsolescence of treaties and of 'conditions whose continuance might endanger the peace of the world',[34] which left open the door to the renegotiation of the Treaty of Versailles. And, most important of all, there was the concept of collective security, derived from the tough-minded thinking of such bodies as the League to Enforce Peace during the war years. Isolationism was dead: any war or threat of war anywhere was recognised as a matter of concern to the League. If any state resorted to

---

32 Loc. cit.
33 R.H.S. Crossman in E.F.M. Durbin, ed., *War and Democracy* (London 1938), p. 278.
34 Viscount Cecil in Leonard Woolf ed. *The Intelligent Man's Way to Prevent War* (London 1933), p. 295.

war in default of its obligation, provision was made for its coercion. Members were obligated to contribute to economic and financial sanctions against it, while the contribution of naval and military force would be a matter for recommendation by the Council. All this was in accordance with the Gladstonian concept of international relations: there *was* a public law of nations, and if need be it should be supported by armed force.

As to whether military sanctions should be used as part of the League's armoury there was understandable controversy. A considerable element insisted that the League was a body which existed to prevent war rather than to wage it, and that it would be ludicrous to provide 'New Wars for Old'.[35] Lord Cecil himself, when he expounded the Covenant to the House of Commons in July 1919, emphasised that there could be 'no attempt to rely upon force to carry out a decision of the Council or the Assembly of the League. That is almost impracticable as things stand now. What we rely upon is public opinion... and if we are wrong about that, the whole thing is wrong.'[36] Very creditably, to obtain clarification of this point was one of their main objects in organising in April 1934 the rather inappropriately named 'Peace Ballot'.[37]

This asked among others the crucial question: 'Do you consider that, if a nation insists on attacking another, the other nations should combine to compel it to stop by (a) economic and non-military measures? (b) if necessary, military measures?

To this eleven and a half million people replied—more than half the total of votes which would be cast in the General Election the following year. To the first part of the question, ninety per cent of the answers were in the affirmative; to the second, slightly over half declared their support for military measures. Only twenty per

---

35 See e.g. H.M. Swanwick, *New Wars for Old* (London 1934).
36 Quoted in E.H. Carr, *The Twenty Years' Crisis* (2nd edn. London 1946), p. 35.
37 Not to be confused with the 'Peace Pledge' which 120,000 people signed by spring 1938: 'We renounce war and never again will we support or sanction another.'

cent returned a firm 'no'.[38] It was a remarkable manifestation of that public opinion in which Bentham had placed so much confidence and which had so repeatedly let down his disciples; and it no doubt encouraged the National Government, when it went to the country the following October, to declare that 'the League of Nations will remain the keystone of British foreign policy.'

But no less important was the attitude of the Labour Party. In 1933 the Party Conference had supported a motion introduced by Sir Charles Trevelyan, pledging the Labour Movement 'to take no part in war and to resist it with the whole force of the Labour Movement'; and further to consider 'what steps, including a general strike, are to be taken to organise the opposition of the organised working-class movement in the event of war or threat of war'[39]—that proposal of Gustav Hervé which had been so universally condemned by the Second International before 1914. Support came from two quarters. There were the absolute pacifists and war-resisters headed by the party's leader, George Lansbury; and there were what might be described as the unreconstructed socialists, those who clung to the Hobson-Leninist theory that war arose simply from the clash of rival imperialisms which in their turn derived from the inherent contradictions of capitalism. The intellectual leader of this group was the immensely prolific Professor Harold Laski, who stated its creed succinctly: 'Foreign investment begat imperialism; imperialism begat militarism; militarism begat war... Once the imperialistic phase has arrived, the relationship between capitalism and war is inescapable.'[40] Or, as Bernard Shaw put it, 'This hideous war of 1914–18 was at bottom a fight between the Capitalists of England, France and Italy on the one side and of those of Germany on the other for command of the African markets.'[41]

The political leader of this group was Sir Stafford Cripps, a man of much the same social background as Sir Charles Trevelyan. He

---

38 D.P. Waley, *British Public Opinion and the Abyssinian War* (London 1975), p. 20.
39 Naylor, *Labour's International Policy*, p. 58.
40 Leonard Woolf, ed., *The Intelligent Man's Way to Prevent War*, p. 505.
41 Quoted in Norman Angell, *After All* (London 1951), p. 141.

saw in the League of Nations nothing but the tool of the satiated capitalist powers. Wars, he wrote, arose out of the struggle for economic power between property-owners and workers, and 'it is as part of this struggle that acts of aggression and war are committed.' 'The competitive necessities of rival capitalist groups may permit of times of truce between wars, but cannot create the atmosphere or temper of peace.'[42] The true economic foundation for peace lay in the common interest of the world's workers, and 'we must start by creating a government in Great Britain that reflects faithfully those desires. Such a government must be under the control of the common people.'[43] Here again we have the simple, arresting doctrine of Tom Paine: there can be no peace in the world until revolutions have brought into power the only people—that is, 'the people'—who genuinely desire peace.

Simple and arresting as it was, it was hardly appropriate for its times. At the 1933 Conference Ernest Bevin, a man of the people if ever there was one, pointed this out rather clearly. A general strike against war? he asked: 'Who and what is there to strike? Trade Unionism has been destroyed in Italy and Germany; practically it does not exist in France; it is extremely weak in the USA... while there is no possibility of a General Strike against the Russian government in the event of war. What is left? Great Britain, Sweden, Denmark and Holland.'[44] A few months later the socialist party of Austria was to be crushed in Vienna by the howitzers of the Dollfuss government. The Labour leadership rapidly re-assessed the situation in the light of the darkening scene in Europe, and came firmly down on the side of Gladstone against Paine, on the side of the League and collective security. In 1934 they reversed the party conference's decision of the previous year by a card vote of three to one. The party accepted instead a report which insisted on the Government's obligation to settle all its disputes by peaceful means; which refused to support the Government if it were condemned by the League as an aggressor or if it became involved in war after refusing arbitration; but which

---

42 Stafford Cripps, *The Struggle for Peace* (London 1936), p. 71-2.
43 Ibid. p. 83.
44 Naylor, *Labour's International Policy*, p. 73.

proclaimed the duty 'unflinchingly to support our Government in all the risks and consequences of fulfilling its duty to take part in collective action against a peace-breaker.' They recognised in fact that:

> there might be circumstances under which the Government of Great Britain might have to use its military and naval forces in support of the League in restraining an aggressor nation which declined to submit to the authority of the League and which flagrantly used military measures in defiance of its pledged word.[45]

A year later, in Spetember 1935, when the Abyssinian crisis had brought the issue down from the realm of abstract ideals to that of practical politics, the Party Conference reaffirmed its determination. A motion affirming Labour's readiness, in co-operation with other nations, 'to use all measures provided under the Covenant to restrain Italy and uphold the League's authority'[46] was passed, over the opposition of both Lansbury and Cripps and after the longest debate in Labour Party history, by 2,168,000 votes to 102,000—a majority of ninety-five per cent.

These decisions, as Clement Attlee was to put it,[47]

> based Labour's foreign policy on the collective peace system through the League of Nations... It rejected the theory of the Balance of Power and demanded the subordination of national sovereignty to world obligations... It linked disarmament with collective security and accepted the obligation to use armed force if necessary in restraining an aggressor State.

It is important to see this not as windy rhetoric—an activity for which Attlee was not renowned—but as the considered statement of a clear, constructive and widely held philosophy. On the one hand was the old system of governments pursuing their self-interest, engaging in secret dimplomacy, forming alliances, piling up armaments, manipulating a balance of power, leading their peoples through exploitation of their patriotic sentiments into a succession of increasingly destructive wars. On the other was a community of like-minded nations, their governments responsive to public opinion, co-operating for their mutual benefit, scaling down their armaments, settling their

---

45 Ibid. pp. 74-5.
46 Ibid. p. 109.
47 Clement Attlee, *The Labour Party in Perspective* (London 1937), p. 153.

differences like reasonable men, enjoying peace under a law which, if need be, they would pool their resources to enforce. It was this vision of collective security that inspired at least some of the undergraduates in the Oxford Union who in February 1933 supported the famous resolution that 'This House would refuse under any circumstances to fight for King and Country.' They did not refuse to fight at all; and when six years later most of them did fight, it was not from the motives of atavistic patriotism which that phrase conjures up, but in the belief, justified or unjustified, that they were defending the basic principles of international law that bound societies together.[48]

But no sooner was this national consensus reached on the principle of collective security—a principle to which the Natinal Government committed itself in the election of 1935—than it was tested; and no sooner was it tested than it failed. And it failed, as its supporters quite rightly discerned, because the government, in spite of their public declarations, remained committed to the traditional way of conducting internataional affairs. Now that the documents are available and we can see the grounds on which they reached their decisions, it is hard to see how they could have done anything else.

On the face of it, the Abyssinian crisis presented not only a clear case but an easy one. One member of the League, Italy, had committed a clear act of aggressive war against another, Abyssinia, with barely an attempt at self-justification, let alone recourse to arbitration procedures. There was none of the ambiguity which attended the Manchurian crisis of 1931. Moreover the aggressor was highly vulnerable to international sanctions, in particular to economic blockade and to naval action. His lines of communication could be severed by the Royal Navy whenever it wished. If he reacted by a declaration of war his naval forces could be quickly crushed. The imposition of sanctions was not only virtually mandatory under the Covenant: it appeared a perfectly practicable and effective course of action—to everybody, that is, outside Whitehall.

From Whitehall the view was different. Sir Maurice Hankey, the immensely influential Secretary of the Cabinet and of the Committee

---

48 See R.B. McCallum, *Public Opinion and the Last Peace* (Oxford University Press 1944), pp. 177-9.

of Imperial Defence, records an interesting discussion which he held on 25 November with Sir Samuel Hoare. Now that the Government had won the election, Hankey suggested,

> they no longer had to angle for votes from the Left Wing and could do what they liked. Hoare said this would be letting down the League. Public opinion would not stand it.[49] I disagreed. All the official world outside the Foreign Office (and many within it) are against sanctions and especially the oil sanction. Most intelligent people outside that I had met felt the same. He said, in effect, that the official world had 'cold feet' about it. I replied in effect that we knew the facts.[50]

'We knew the facts'! That cold, unanswerable statement with which bureaucrats always floor their critics! What were these facts? Briefly, that ever since 1931 British defence planners had been concerned about the vulnerability of British possessions in the Far East to attack by the Japanese Navy. They relied on having a capital fleet capable of sailing to Singapore to deter and if necessary combat such attack. Second, ever since 1933 they had been concerned about the revival of German military power, and the French had been even more concerned. Prudence dictated that Italy should not be unnecessarily antagonised, and if possible should be won over as an ally. If war came, Hankey told Hoare:

> Although we should probably beat Italy, we might sustain some serious losses of warships (from aircraft and submarine attack for example) and... in view of the obscure attitude of Japan in the Far East and German rearmament in the West, we cannot afford to weaken ourselves by such a futile war, or to make a permanent enemy of a nation that lies athwart our main line of communication to the Far East.

These were the arguments of the old system—exactly those calculations based on the balance of power which the liberal conscience found so immoral. Attlee had already expressed his concern about

---

49 Considering that barely ten weeks had elapsed since Hoare had at Geneva declared that Britain stood 'for the collective maintenance of the Covenant in its entirety and particularly for steady and collective resistance to all acts of unprovoked aggression', this was the least he could say. (Waley, *British Public Opinion*, p.38.)

50 S.W. Roskill, *Hankey, Man of Secrets* (London 1974), vol. III, p. 187.

them in the Hosue of Commons. 'What has distrubed me in recent years,' he said in July 1935, 'is that in all these discussions about the position of Abyssinia and so forth, what has concerned us most has been, not so much what is right, as what will be the effect on something else in connection with foreign affairs.'[51] Attlee and his colleagues had no doubts as to what was right, and the extent to which public opinion supported them was revealed over the affair of the Hoare–Laval Pact. This attempt to pacify Italy by concessions at the expense of Abyssinia aroused a storm of protest which provides an interesting contrast with the wave of relief that swept the country when Mr Chamberlain negotiated a very similar settlement at Munich three years later. A bewildered Samuel Hoare was sacrificed (rather briefly) to appease it; but it was to be the view of Hankey and his colleagues that prevailed.

Thus, over the Abyssinian crisis we find the two concepts we have been discussing, collective security and balance of power, in direct confrontation. The first commanded the support of most articulate public opinion; the latter was to prevail. But it was the first, the voice of the liberal conscience, that now counselled war; the second, the voice of the government, the officials, the despised 'establishment', that courted public and international humiliation to preserve peace.

The pattern was shortly to be repeated.

---

51 Naylor, *Labour's International Policy*, p. 92.

5
THE CHALLENGE OF FASCISM 1935–1945

In the last chapter we attempted to trace what had happened to the various strands of British Liberal thinking about war and international politics as a result of the First World War. Tom Paine's doctrine, that peace could be brought about only by revolution, was now the accepted view of the left wing of the Labour Party, with Harold Laski as its most forceful expounder, Stafford Cripps as its political standard bearer, the indefatigable and now sexagenarian Sir Charles Trevelyan outdoing the most violent of his juniors in his commitment to the cause. The Mazzinian doctrine, that peace could result only from national self-determination, had left its followers in disarray. It had caused chaos at the Paris peace conference, and it was increasingly clear that this mode of thought lent itself far more readily to right-wing authoritarianism, not least to Mussolini's Fascist movement and its more powerful imitator north of the Alps, than it did to any form of parliamentary democracy. Certainly it provided no answer to the problem of international order, as Norman Angell pointed out in his book *The Unseen Assassins* in 1932. The international anarchy, he wrote,[1]

is not created by Capitalism, nor would it be solved by Socialism. And Socialist States which were also Nationalist would have even more cause for quarrel than States which permit individuals to form economic organisations which are often in fact international, which function in large degree irrespective of national barriers.

---

1 Norman Angell, *The Unseen Assassins*, p. 201.

The remedy, in fact, said Angell, was 'not Nationalism, which threatens to Balkanise the world, but Internationalism'[2]: the answer to war lay in self-knowledge, in education, and in the creation of international institutions; the view which inspired the mainstream of liberal thinking in the interwar years and underlay the whole concept of collective security. But whereas in the 1920s there had been wide support for Bentham's assumption that the only guarantee needed for such security lay in the power of public opinion,[3] by the mid-1930s this belief was no longer tenable. The behaviour of the Japanese in Manchuria, and Hitler's rise to power in Germany had, even before the Abyssinian crisis, foreshadowed the problems to come and made Gladstone's stern injunctions as to the need and duty, if need be, to enforce against transgressors, laws based on the civilised consensus of mankind, seem rather more relevant than Bentham's serene assurances that such enforcement ought never to be necessary.

We saw in the last chapter how broad was the consensus behind this concept of collective security, how widely it was regarded as a new ordering of international society, as a serious and practicable alternative to the bad old ways of arms races and the balance of power. Leonard Woolf defined it in 1933 as 'a universal world order, an ordered society of nations in which if there is a dispute over "rights", right is not determined by the relative military strength of the disputants, but by the impartial conciliation or decision of those who are not party to the dispute. In such an ordered society of nations ... it is essential that each nation should look for security against aggression, not to the strength of its own arms and allies ... but to the whole society of nations, the collective guarantee and pooled security of all nations.'[4] This was the philosophy behind the 'Peace Ballot' of 1934, the view endorsed by both the Labour and Liberal Parties and apparently adopted by the National Government in the election of 1935; only to be betrayed a few months later by the Hoare–Laval Pact. The evil old philosophy, that looked to armaments, power-balances

---

2 Ibid. p. 203.
3 See E.H. Carr, *The Twenty Year Crisis*, p. 34–6.
4 Leonard Woolf, *The Intelligent Man's Way to Prevent War* (London 1933), p. 12.

and secret diplomacy to keep the peace and which had so repeatedly failed, now appeared in spite of all the hopes of the 1920s, in spite of the Covenant of the League and the Kellogg Pact, to be as firmly in the saddle as ever.

Thereafter, the brief consensus which had united the Government and its opponents disappeared. The Abyssinian crisis, as Kingsley Martin was to write, 'marks the dividing line in the Thirties. After that the one hope that England would stand for a constructive world policy came to an end.'[5] On this the perception of the liberals was quite correct. Whereas they were trying to create a new rule of law, the government was indeed attempting to create a balance of power, an alignment of status-quo orientated powers which would, they hoped, hold in check the revisionist claims of Germany and Japan. The first course meant condemning Italy, the second conciliating her. The first course involved at least a risk of war with Italy, though many of its advocates preferred to overlook it; but for the government, such a conflict would be, as was later to be said (under very comparable circumstances) of the Korean War, the wrong war, in the wrong place, at the wrong time, against the wrong enemy.

From 1934 onwards, the British Chiefs of Staff had seen the main long-term threat to international security to lie in the revival of German military power. But for the great majority of liberals, the Germans were a deeply-wronged people whose claims to a revision of the Treaty of Versailles were deserving of unstinted support. When in March 1935 Hitler reintroduced conscription into Germany, the Labour *Daily Herald* welcomed it as a sign that Europe was 'bright with hope' since 'the poison of Versailles is at least draining from its blood'.[6] And when a year later Hitler denounced the Locarno Treaties and reoccupied the Rhineland, Hugh Dalton told the House of Commons, 'the Labour Party would not support the taking of military sanctions or even economic sanctions against Germany'; and that a distinction must be drawn 'between the action of Signor Mussolini in resorting to aggressive war and waging it beyond his frontiers, and the actions ... of Herr Hitler which, much as we regard

---

5 Kingsley Martin, *Editor* (London 1968), p. 178.
6 Quoted in Waley, *British Public Opinion & the Abyssinian War*, p. 27.

them as reprehensible, have taken place within the frontiers of the Third Reich'.[7] The Left in fact, even those who like Dalton himself accepted the need for enforcement of collective security, still refused to abandon their fundamental principles and think in terms of the calculus of military power.

Against those who did so think, those ministers and officials whose ideas remained rooted in a world of national rivalries and armaments and alliances, the Labour Party closed its ranks. The Service Estimates were unanimously opposed by the Labour Party: by the left wing because they put arms in the hands of the class enemy, and by the moderates because those arms would not be used in accordance with those principles of collective security in which alone they saw salvation. In February 1936 the *New Statesman* wrote with some accuracy that the Government wanted arms only 'because ... [it] does not believe in the League and knows that Europe is returning to the old system of the Balance of Power'; and it drew the conclusion, in June, that Labour should 'refuse, and ask everyone to refuse, support of a rearmament designed not for genuine collective security but for a balance of power policy which means war.' The Parliamentary Labour Party took this advice, explaining its opposition to the Service Estimates in terms of 'its entire opposition to the international policy of the Government, of which the rearmament programme is an integral part'.[8] The position was explained perhaps most lucidly by the leader of the Party, Clement Attlee, in his testament *The Labour Party in Perspective*, published in 1937:[9]

> The Labour Party ... can only tolerate armaments as a necessary support for a policy of collective security. It is fully alive to the dangers which exist in Europe, owing to the aggressive policy of the fascist powers, but it has no confidence in the will of the capitalist government to oppose them. There is every indication that the policy pursued is an attempt to play the old game of 'alliances' based on the maintenance of the balance of power. To say that what the Government is doing is necessary for the defence of the country is to beg the whole question. I do not believe that the entry into an arms race

---

7   Naylor, *Labour's International Policy*, p. 132.
8   Ibid. pp. 149–53.
9   C.R. Attlee, *The Labour Party in Perspective* (London 1937), p. 190.

would give security. On the contrary I think it is leading us straight to the disaster of another World War.

So war and national defence, the activities for which the British Government was now reluctantly planning, were regarded by the Labour Party as being totally different from the course it wanted to pursue: 'the enforcement of collective security' and 'resistance to Fascism'. The liberal conscience in the mid-thirties was equally revolted by war and by Fascism, and so found it easy to believe that the two were one and the same: that opposition to the one involved opposing the other. In July the International Meeting of the Trades Union Congress in London issued a ringing declaration:[10]

Considering ... that Fascism is eager to destroy human liberties and the rights of workers all over the world, to crush the workers' organisations and democracies, the International Trades Union Meeting reiterates that Fascism must be combated in every country, with all possible means... *Everything must be done to hurl back the forces of Fascism and to stem the tide of war.* [my italics].

'Against Fascism and War' became a slogan behind which the entire forces of the Left could rally, and to vote against rearmament could be depicted as a vote against Fascism. Support for the Government's rearmament policy, Attlee told the Labour Party Conference in October 1936, 'will lead you to demand after demand being made on your liberties. It will, in effect, lead to a demand that you shall accept Fascism practically, in order to conquer Fascism.'[11]

Even those who could not seriously identify the British government as Fascist (and there were many of the Left who could and did) did not believe that it had any serious intention of *fighting* Fascism. To quote Attlee again:

Although they fear the Fascist States, they dread still more the workers who are the effective force against Fascism... It is impossible for a Government which believes in inequality at home to support effective equality abroad. It is no accident that the Government which has betrayed peace and democracy abroad should have as its emblem and symbol the Means Test.

---

10 K.W. Watkins, *Britain Divided: the Effect of the Spanish Civil War on British Public Opinion* (London 1936), p. 146.

11 Naylor, op. cit. p. 160.

Here again we have the spirit of Tom Paine, which reigned almost supreme in the Labour Party from 1936 until 1939: no just international order would be possible until the rotten gang in charge at home had been swept away. But it was no longer assumed that world peace would then automatically follow. On the contrary: the hands of the British working class would then be freed to join with their fellow toilers abroad in the struggle against the forces of Fascism—especially as manifested in Spain.

For during the course of 1936 liberal perceptions of the international scene had very radically changed. Expectation of collective security under the aegis of the League of Nations had, after the Abyssinian crisis, dwindled almost to nothing. Their place was taken by an apocalyptic vision of a Manichaean, a cosmic struggle between the dark forces of Fascism on the one hand and those of democracy on the other; a transnational conflict of ideologies to which neither the old balance of power system nor hopes of collective security had any relevance; a conflict which was coming to a head on the battlefields of Spain.

Fascism took both liberals and socialists by surprise. A few nineteenth-century sages—a Burckhardt, a Nietzsche—had some inkling of the forces that might be unchained in mass industrialised societies, but nothing in the thinking of Bentham and Mill, on the one hand, nor of Marx and Engels on the other had prepared their followers for the emergence of movements which were both populist and authoritarian, which harnessed mass opinion to a militaristic ethic, which were equally hostile to traditional class-structures and to democratic values, and which had no interest whatever in world peace. The slogan 'Fascism means War' was almost tautological: Fascist ideologues never pretended anything else. And into the shades of difference which lay between authoritarian right-wing *régimes* concerned to preserve a social order, such as that of Franco himself, and the radical, nihilistic, destructive philosophies of the National Socialists in Germany, only the most dispassionate of political scientists were concerned to enquire.

Spain thus provided a conveniently unambiguous battlefield for what all shades of liberals and radicals could regard as the most just of all conceivable wars: a war on war itself. 'The struggle in Spain is the world at the cross-roads,' Harry Pollitt wrote in August 1936:[12] 'The signs are clearly pointed—democracy and peace, or fascism and war.' The emotions aroused were much the same as we have seen in our own time over Allende's Chile: a government freely elected by full democratic process, a government openly dedicated to the cause of the workers, had come under assault from forces of reaction covertly aided by foreign powers. Some sympathisers stressed the continuity with nineteenth-century struggles. The forces of reaction in Spain— Church, Nobility, Army—were, after all, the same enemies against which Mazzini, Garibaldi and their followers had fought for so long. 'It was the hope of liberation from ancient tyranny that inspired resistance to Franco...' wrote Kingsley Martin. 'The issue was whether Spain must for ever remain a backward, uneducated, impoverished land under the autocratic rule of priests and the army.'[13]

Many young Englishmen of the upper classes went to fight in Spain consciously in the spirit of Lord Byron. Stephen Spender was one. 'I support Spain,' he wrote, 'exactly such a movement in liberal and liberating nationalism as the English liberals supported in many countries all groaning under feudalism in the nineteenth century.'[14] Others, working-class militants, saw Spain as a battleground where they could work out the class struggle which they believed to be universal and only latent within their own community.[15] The fight against Fascism in Spain was for them the same fight that had to be waged against the forces of reaction and oppression at home. But in Spain the enemy was visible and accessible. You could shoot at him.

Finally there were other ardent spirits who sought release from a more generalised malaise. In an anthology on conscientious objection, published before the Spanish Civil War even began, Julian Bell, one of the young Cambridge intellectuals who was to die in Spain, wrote:[16]

---

12 Quoted in Watkins, op. cit. p. 148.
13 Kingsley Martin, *Editor*, p. 211.
14 Samuel Hayes, *The Auden Generation* (London 1976), p. 263.
15 Watkins, op. cit. p. 172.
16 Julian Bell, ed. *We Did Not Fight*, quoted in Hynes, op. cit. p. 195.

The most active and ardent war resisters—at least among my own generation and those of military age—are more likely to take the line of revolutionary action than conscientious objection ... Those of us who care about the human race and what happens to it have come to believe that only effective action counts ... I believe that the war resistance movements of my generation will in the end succeed in putting down war—by force if necessary.

So these young men went to Spain as their elders had gone to Flanders two decades earlier: to die in a war against war.

For the techniques and activities of the traditional Peace Movement these radicals had no sympathy whatever. Kingsley Martin attended a *Rassemblement universelle pour la Paix* in Brussels in September 1937 and wrote of it afterwards:[17]

I quite lost my temper at this preposterous conference. I looked at Lord Cecil's superb profile in the chair, and at Philip Noel Baker at his side, drafting, translating, dauntless and always optimistic; I heard professional League of Nations speakers talking about the value of congresses helping us 'to appreciate each other's difficulties and points of view' and courageously pretending that there was still such a thing as collective security ... The Congress even invented a Peace Day, a Peace Fair, and a Peace Party ... There was a Peace Oath too, but the Oath, like everything else, carefully avoided the only question that mattered—whether pacifists would or would not fight against aggressions ...

For the radicals therefore, 'peace' became a dirty word, and 'appeasement' of course, a dirtier one. To stand aside from this struggle was at best to show oneself to be blind to its implications, at worst to conspire with the enemy.

And stand aside from the struggle was of course exactly what the British Government tried to do. In terms of ideology it had little sympathy with the Left. In terms of national policy and planning it had no wish to get involved in yet another conflict in the wrong place at the wrong time, even if not now the wrong enemy. The Chiefs of Staff may not have been concerned with fighting Fascism, but they were very much concerned with the problem of fighting Germany, and in view of the appalling disparity of air power they felt in no condition to do so yet. The Cabinet itself was profoundly reluctant to fight anyone; and by 1937, when it was clear that they faced not some

---

17 Kinglsey Martin, *Editor*, p. 219.

swift, efficient police-action against a minor power, but a major war in which British cities would be heavily at risk, they were probably not unrepresentative of the bulk of British public opinion.

And with regard to Germany, had not the British public been educated by the radicals themselves to recognise the justice of her claims to rehabilitation, to *Gleichberechtigung*? We have seen how the men who were the most hostile to the old balance of power system, those who were the most energetic in promoting the cause of collective security, tended quite naturally to be those most concerned to right the wrongs done to Germany. Clifford Allen, the heroic conscientious objector of the Great War, a truly saintly figure in the Labour Party, had as early as May 1933 urged his colleagues not to be misled by Nazi atrocities:[18]

> So profound is our horror at the almost unbelievable brutalities which are now taking place in Germany that we are in danger of letting our indignation on that subject lead us to false and even dangerous thinking on other aspects of the German problem. Germany is but little interested either in rearming or disarming: her one concern is to secure equality.

For the next five years Allen and those who thought like him made increasingly anguished attempts to reconcile their desire to redress the wrongs done to the Germans with their horror at what was going on in the Third Reich. They maintained, with Philip Lothian and others, that 'in some degree the brutality of National Socialists is the reaction to the treatment given to Germany herself since the war' and that 'the best way of restoring reasonable rights to the Jews in Germany is not to counter hate with hate, but to undermine the source of the evil aspects of National Socialism by giving Germany her rightful place in Europe.'[19] J.A. Hobson wrote to Allen in January 1937:[20]

> I feel that nothing can be done until 'International Relations' are put on a safe footing. And among these relations I believe that our attitude to the

---

18 Martin Gilbert, *Plough My Own Furrow: the Story of Lord Allen of Hurtwood* (London 1965), p. 351.
19 Lothian letter of 1 February 1935, quoted in Martin Gilbert, *Britain & Germany between the Wars* (London 1964), p. 78.
20 Gilbert, op. cit. p. 380.

German demand for Colonies blocks all progress. To say that Germany can have access to raw materials without colonies and that we cannot return her former colonies or find any substitute without the formal consent of the inhabitants of such areas, cannot be expected to satisfy any 'have not' country.

Coming from the originator of the doctrine that it was primarily the clash of rival European imperialisms that caused wars, this comment is interesting, to put it no more strongly. But rather less out of character was Hobson's letter to the *Manchester Guardian* on 10 May 1938 at the time of the first Czech crisis of that year:[21]

Czecho-Slovakia has never been a nation in any intelligible sense; the pretence that it is was one of the worst follies of the post-war treaty ... Czechoslovakia as a State would not be injured by the withdrawal of a permanently dissatisfied German minority, and though Germany might gain in numbers, territory and industry, is that a proper ground for any further interference on our part?

The argument from nationality was thus favourable to the appeasement of Germany, even if that from the rights of small states was not; while arguments based on the balance of power could be ignored. Kingsley Martin agreed. In August 1938 in a famous leader in the *New Statesman* he suggested that 'the Czechs [should] make an imaginative offer of partnership to the Sudeten Germans, to reconcile them to existing frontiers. But if ... this is impossible, the question of frontier revision, difficult though it is, should at once be tackled. The strategical value of the Bohemian frontier should not be made the occasion of a world war.'[22] Clifford Allen himself spent the last months of his life and the last ounce of his strength in devising and popularising a formula for the peaceful cession of the Sudetenland to Germany under international guarantee. On 7 October 1938 he was able to write to a colleague: 'It is lovely to think that the actual formula for the Four Power Conference which we worked out and put to Ribbentrop when we were in Berlin, should have been the instrument which saved the peace of the world.'[23] He died five

---

21 Quoted in Gilbert, op. cit. p. 400.
22 In C.H. Rolph, *Kingsley: the Life...of Kingsley Martin* (London 1973), p. 245.
23 Gilbert, op. cit. p. 415.

months later still a happy man; but only just. Twelve days after his death, Hitler entered Prague.

Thus appeasement, no less than the struggle against Fascism, was the product of the liberal conscience, and the two sentiments could cohabit within the same breast. They did, for example, in that of Kingsley Martin, who, in spite of his belief that the Czechs should yield their frontier rather than provoke war, wrote in the *New Statesman* in March 1938:[24]

> It is time that the people of England told Mr Chamberlain in unmistakable language that for a policy of connivance and encouragement to Fascism the British nation is not prepared for more taxation, for more conscription or for discipline, but that there is no sacrifice it is not prepared to undergo for a government which really intends to throw its weight on the side of democracy and against aggression.

It was a terrible problem for the truly conscientious. Should Germany's wrongs be righted, at risk of strengthening Fascism? But if her wrongs *were* righted, might this not *weaken* Fascism? If the German people had restored to them the rights and territories of which they had been deprived by the Versailles Settlement, would not they rejoin the comity of peace-loving powers, and their militarism wither away?

In general, however, in the last two years before the war, the liberal conscience was militant rather than appeasing. After 1937 the Labour Party in the House of Commons ceased its opposition to the annual Service Estimates, even if it now supported them only out of a sense of self-preservation. As Dalton told the Party Conference in October 1937, 'A British Labour Government, coming to power tomorrow, would be in danger of humiliations, intimidations and acts of foreign intervention in our national affairs which it is not tolerable for Englishmen to contemplate.'[25] There were of course still those who saw the fight against Fascism in terms, not of a national war between the democracies and the Axis powers, but of the international and internal class struggle; who drew no distinction between the capitalist enemy at home and the Fascist enemy abroad, and saw no contradiction in demanding arms for Spain and opposing arms

---

24 K. Martin, *Editor*, p. 249.
25 Naylor, op. cit. p. 200.

for Britain. 'We are prepared,' said the young Aneurin Bevan at the same Conference,

to make whatever sacrifices are necessary, to give whatever arms are necessary in order to fight Fascist Powers and in order to consolidate world peace ... [but] we are not going to put a sword in the hands of our enemies that may be used to cut off our own hands.[26]

But by a ten to one majority their objections were defeated.

Hitler's destruction of Czechoslovakia in March 1939 was to re-establish a national consensus as wide as, and considerably more lasting than, that which had appeared to exist in the summer of 1935 over the issue of collective security. The last illusion, that the appeasement of Germany's legitimate grievances would restore stability to Europe, had been stripped away. The traditionalists, Churchill at their head, were prepared to fight as they had fought in 1914 and quite often before that, to prevent an accumulation of hostile power on the Continent so great as to destroy Britain's capacity for independent action—for blunt motives, in fact, of power politics; but it was not only traditionalists who were now prepared to think in these terms. As Norman Angell was ruefully to confess in his autobiography, although 'Balance of Power had a bad smell with nearly all Liberals, including this one ... later on [they] came to see that power politics were the politics of not being overpowered.'[27] Gladstonian Liberals could again feel that the public law of Europe was at stake, challenged as much by Hitler's domestic atrocities as by his infringements of the rights of other sovereign States; and that an obligation rested upon the United Kingdom to act even if there existed no Concert of Powers to condemn him. For the latter-day Mazzinians, no clearer case could have been presented than the destruction of Czechoslovakia, and later of Poland, for the need to defend the independence of small nations. For the defenders of democracy and the cause of the workers against Fascism it was simply an extension of the struggle which had been gathering momentum since the murder of Matteotti, and in which so many of them had already died in Spain. Only those stalwarts of the British Communist Party who uncritically followed

---

26 Ibid.
27 Norman Angell, *After All* (London 1951), p. 137.

the directives of Moscow adhered to the line, abandoned now even by Cripps and Trevelyan, that this was simply another imperialist struggle arising out of the contradictions of capitalism. By doing so they forfeited all serious influence on British public opinion for a quarter of a century to come.

So yet again the liberal conscience endorsed a national struggle as a just war. There were some radicals who found themselves ill at ease in the traditionalist company they had to keep, who felt that there was something wrong in being taught how to fight for democracy by drill-sergeants on the barrack square, under an officer-class which expressed little sympathy for their political views. This, they sometimes felt, was not really *their* war. One or two felt it so strongly that they preferred to watch at a comfortable distance from the other side of the Atlantic. But the proof of the pudding lay in the eating: in the aims for which the war was fought and the peace which emerged at the end of it.

The declaration of Allied objectives made by Neville Chamberlain immediately on the outbreak of the war was irreproachable. 'In this war,' he said, 'we are not fighting against the German people, for whom we have no bitter feelings, but against a tyrannous and foresworn *régime*'; and a month later, 'We are aiming not only at victory but rather look beyond it to the laying of a foundation of a better international system ... I am certain that all the peoples of Europe, including the peoples of Germany, long for peace.'[28] Here we have the pure doctrine of the eighteenth-century philosophers; all peoples desire peace, only their rulers drag them into wars. Naturally the Labour Party agreed: it was Nazism, rather than Germany, that had to be overthrown. *The New Statesman* heartily applauded the dropping of leaflets, rather than bombs, over Germany on pure Benthamite grounds: 'To enlighten the German people about the behaviour of their rulers,' wrote Kingsley Martin, 'is the most important of all the tasks before us.'[29] The belief died hard that 'the German people'

---

28 Quoted in John Wheeler Bennett and A.J. Nicholls, *The Semblance of Peace* (London 1972), p. 14.

29 Quoted in T.D. Burridge, *British Labour and Hitler's War* (London 1976), p. 24.

were, like all peoples, almost by definition good, and with sufficient encouragement might be persuaded to liberate themselves from their militaristic leaders and reveal themselves to be as rational, democratic and peace-loving as their English friends and helpers.

That there *were* such men and women in Germany is a matter of record. But by 1940 the most courageous of them were already in concentration camps and the political effectiveness of those who were not made the arguments of their supporters seem, as the war went on, increasingly unconvincing. It grew ever harder to maintain that Europe had been conquered and policed, and that the Jews were being exterminated by the million, by an unrepresentative minority against the wishes of 'the German people'. It was also harder to maintain, in a wartime Britain which revealed a remarkable degree of underlying social cohesion, that the war was an international crusade against a Fascist adversary whose ranks included, alike and indistinguishable, Nazi *gauleiters* and English civil servants, the Gestapo and the Metropolitan Police. After 22 June 1941, when the Soviet Union entered the war, not even the British Communist Party attempted to maintain it. It became accepted as much on the Left as on the Right that this was a war specifically against *Germany*, against a philosophy which appeared to be distinctively German and one which inspired a depressingly high proportion of the German people. In November 1941 even Aneurin Bevan wrote that 'it was Prussian militarism, with all its terrible philosophy, that had to be got rid of from Europe for all time'; and the following September the President of the TUC told his annual conference 'that until the German people, not alone their gangster rulers, have meted out to them what they have meted out to millions of their fellow creatures ... the German people will again, if not prevented, make another attempt to enslave Europe.'[30]

This time there was little if any radical sympathy for the attitude adopted during the First World War by the Union for Democratic Control: that immediately after the war Germany should be rehabilitated and treated as an equal. There was considerable doubt as to whether Germany as a nation should be permitted to survive at all, and no doubt whatever that 'the German people' would need a

---

30 Burridge, op. cit. pp. 60–4.

prolonged period of control and re-education. In July 1943 Clement Attlee wrote a memorandum to the Cabinet which insisted that 'very positive action will have to be taken by the victorious powers if there is to be a new orientation of the German nation'; and what was required was spelled out in a report which the National Executive Committee of the Labour Party submitted to the Annual Conference the following April and which was accepted by a large majority. Germany should be completely disarmed and occupied for a considerable period; the power of the Junkers, the military castes and industrialists should be broken; Germany's economy should be put under international control, her war potential was to be reduced and was to make full reparation and restitution to those she had plundered. 'A great moral and mental revolution' would be needed, said Attlee, before the Germans could be trusted again; and, as he told the House of Commons, 'it was idle to think that the process of converting the Germans from the barbarities into which they had sunk to civilisation was not going to take a long time.'[31]

By 1945 therefore, liberal thinkers in England had embraced the position which Thorstein Veblen had set out so starkly some thirty years earlier: the Germans must be forced to be free and compulsorily educated in how to be so. Democracy only made for peace when all states were equally democratic, and those which *were* democratic had to remould in their own image, forcibly if necessary, those which were not. There was nothing very new about this: the enthusiasts of the French Revolution, finding the peoples of Europe reluctant to accept the liberties brought to them on the points of French bayonets, had felt much the same. Opposing elites had to be eliminated; the likeminded and reliable had to be put in positions of responsibility and supported; the religious and educational system had to be controlled and if need be changed.

In Veblen's own country there was less emphasis on the re-education of the German people, a long-term task which the United States was prepared to leave to its Allies. There the stress was laid rather on their punishment, and on the reduction or elimination of the power of the German State, whether by partition of pasto-

---

31 Ibid. pp. 94, 118, 154.

ralisation. The approach was moralistic and legalistic: Germany had committed outrages against international law and morality and must suffer the consequences. Roosevelt spoke at Tehran about the need 'to drive home to the German people the fact that they had lost the war and had been engaged in lawless conspiracy against the decencies of civilisation.'[32] The principal conspirators had to be arraigned, indicted, and subjected to due process of law. The Morgenthau Plan for the pastoralisation of Germany commanded little support, for practical rather than for humanitarian reasons; but there was much sympathy in Washington and elsewhere for the view expressed by the Secretary of State, Cordell Hull,[33] that Germany should be kept under military control, if need be for fifty years, until she experienced an absolute change of heart; and that 'the standard of living of the German population should be kept below the average of neighbouring populations but should be raised gradually in proportion to the rate of change on their part away from Nazism, racial superiority and the like, towards ideas of human rights, individual liberty, freedom and peace.' Retribution and reformation should go hand in hand.

Cordell Hull spoke with a voice which Mr Gladstone would surely have approved. Germany had transgressed against the public law of nations, as much by her internal as by her external crimes. That law had been vindicated by a Concert of peace-loving Powers, no longer European only but now world-wide, the United Nations. The Concert should now be established upon a formal and permanent basis, and Germany and her associates could be admitted to it only after a long process of purging their offences. And this time there must be no mistake: the new organisation, unlike the League of Nations, should be explicitly and unambiguously a league to enforce peace. As Hull had declared in September 1943: 'It is abundantly clear that a system of organised international co-operation for the maintenance of peace must be based upon the willingness of the co-operating nations to use force, if necessary, to keep the peace.'[34] And, as a result of his energetic activities the following month, the Allies

---

32 In Wheeler Bennett and Nicholls, *The Semblance of Peace*, p. 167.
33 Cordell Hull, *Memoirs* (London 1948), vol. II, p. 1617.
34 Ibid. p. 1254.

signed in Moscow a Declaration, by which they agreed to establish a general international organisation, based on the sovereign equality of all nations; for the maintenance of peace and security; which would include provision for military forces to be available to meet a threat to the peace.

So as the war ended in the summer of 1945 the dreams of the *philosophes* seemed at last to be about to come true with establishment of an international organisation truly global in scope and supported, as the League of Nations had never been, by the combined authority of the most powerful states in the world. Cautious European conservatives might see in the United Nations no more than a concert of victorious powers; concerned, as similar concerts after 1815 and 1918 had been concerned, to establish and preserve the distribution of power. But for liberals, especially American liberals, it was a great deal more than that. It was the collective conscience of mankind—and a conscience as much concerned with the internal affairs of nations as with their international relations. The two world wars may have destroyed all illusions about the peace-loving quality of democratic societies, but they had provided sufficient evidence about the belligerent nature of undemocratic societies—the militarism both of Wilhemine and Nazi Germany and of Imperial Japan—for the universalisation of democratic institutions to be seen as a necessary, even if not a sufficient foundation for world peace. Conversely, the object of the new world order was to make possible the extension of democratic governments. Peace and democracy were interdependent.

Such at least was the burden of the successive declarations of Allied governments from 1941 onwards, in which the United States consistently took the lead. By the Atlantic Charter in August 1941 the British and American Governments bound themselves to 'respect the right of all peoples to choose the form of the government under which they will live,' and expressed the wish 'to see sovereign rights and self-government restored to those who have been forcibly deprived of them.' They would recognise 'no territorial changes that do not accord with the freely-expressed wishes of the peoples concerned.' And they intended to establish a peace 'which will afford to all nations the means of dwelling in safety within their own boundaries,' so 'that all the men in all the lands may live out their lives in freedom from fear and want';[35] an aspiration to be epitomised by Roosevelt as 'the Four Freedoms: freedom from Want, freedom from Fear, freedom of Speech, freedom of Religion.' A few months later America had entered the war and on New Year's Day 1942 the combined United Nations rededicated themselves to the defence and preservation of life, liberty, independence and religious freedom and 'to preserve human rights and justice in their own lands as well as other lands.'[36] And most important of all, on 11 February 1945, as their armies were converging on the centre of a shattered Europe, the heads of the American, Soviet and British governments met at Yalta and issued the following Declaration on Liberated Europe:[37]

> The establishment of order in Europe and the rebuilding of economic life must be achieved by processes which will enable the liberated peoples [to destroy the last vestiges of Nazism and Fascism and] to create democratic institutions of their own choice. [The three Governments therefore agreed to assist the liberated European peoples] to form interim governmental authorities broadly representative of all democratic elements in the population and pledged to the earliest possible establishment through free elections of governments responsive to the will of the people.

This declaration, together with the establishment of a United Nations Organisation, whose members were pledged by its Charter 'to take effective collective measures for the prevention and removal of threats to the peace and for the suppression of acts of aggression or other breaches of the peace', provided the firmest possible assurance to liberal thinkers in the Western World that the Second World War had been worth while: that it would not result, as all other wars had resulted, in a return to an anarchy of sovereign states, exacerbated by an arms race and tempered only by a balance of power.

---

35 Wheeler Bennett & Nicholls, op. cit. p. 42.
36 Ibid. p. 537.
37 Ibid. p. 631.

6
THE CHALLENGE OF COMMUNISM 1945–1975

There can have been few people in the Western World (and even fewer in the Soviet Union) who did not believe in 1945 that the war which they had fought and won had been not only necessary but in every sense 'just'. Traditionalists may have seen it as yet another war to restore a balanced system of international politics; the unpolitical masses in Britain and the Soviet Union certainly saw it as a war for sheer survival; but for the liberals, as we have defined them in these pages, it was a war to defend and vindicate all the cultural values for which they had stood since the dawn of the liberal conscience in the eighteenth century; the values of 'democracy' against Fascism, the values of freedom of speech and of worship, of freedom from want and from fear, the values of national self-determination against alien tyranny, the values inherent in the rule of law in the international community, the values of Paine and Bentham and Gladstone and Mazzini all rolled into one. Even that severest of critics, Mr A.J.P. Taylor, concluded his account of it by saying that it was a 'good war'.[1]

Nowhere was this sense of a successful crusade stronger than in the United States. In a unique sense these values were precisely what America was all about; the values to which the Founding Fathers had dedicated their country and which had ever since provided the criteria by which they judged the policy of others and incited their own to be

---

1 A.J.P. Taylor, *The Second World War* (London 1975), p. 234.

judged. In his fascinating book *To the Farewell Address*[2] Dr Felix Gilbert has shown how explicitly George Washington and his generation associated themselves with the ideas of the liberal philosophers of the eighteenth century, with their belief in freedom of opinion and freedom of trade as the guarantees of perpetual peace; and how explicitly they dissociated themselves from the world of balance of power and secret diplomacy and aristocratic militarism which those philosophers denounced. The United States indeed, virtually alone among nations, found and to some extent still finds its identity not so much in ethnic community or shared historical experience as in dedication to a value system: and the reiteration of these values, the repeated proclamation of and dedication to the liberal creed, has always been a fundamental element in the cohesion of American society.

In this respect the United States has always resembled rather a secular church, or perhaps a gigantic sect, than it has the nation-states of the Old World. Like those sects which played so large a part in its foundation, the original concern of the United States had been to keep itself unspotted from the infections of the world, to create an inward-looking community whose members could practise and bear witness to their faith. And again like those sects, which—as we have seen with Quakers—as they grew in wealth and power moved out into the world to evangelise and transform it, so did the United States gradually involve itself in an international system within which it could operate with a clear conscience only it if could remake that system in its own image. The first attempt to do so, by Woodrow Wilson, saw the humiliating failure of a man whose lack of understanding of the international environment was paralleled by his lack of skill in manipulating domestic politics. Franklin Roosevelt could not be faulted on the latter count, whatever one may feel about the former; but in any case, American public opinion had moved fast and far since the days of Senator Lodge. By the end of 1942 a Gallup Poll revealed that nearly seventy-five per cent of the population favoured American participation in a post-war interna-

---

2   Felix Gilbert, *To the Farewell Address: Ideas of Early American Foreign Policy* (Princeton 1961).

tional organisation to keep the peace; and this proportion remained stable until the end of the war.³

But the assumption—and one constantly reiterated by American politicians and publicists at every level—was that this organisation would not be the old balance of power system, the old Concert of Europe writ large. It would be the framework of a new world of peace under law. The successive declarations to which American statesmen and their allies had set their hands, from the Atlantic Charter to the Yalta Declaration on Liberated Europe, were seen not as vague statements of intent but as morally binding obligations on all parties concerned, pledging them to the creation of a new world order: that world of which liberals had dreamed for two hundred years, a world of freedom of speech and assembly and religion, of freedom of movement and of trade. Of course it was seen as a world in which the United States and its citizens would flourish and enrich themselves, and historians of the revisionist school have seen in such aspirations no more than a cloak for American capitalist-imperialistic designs for the domination of the world.⁴ The same accusations had been made, with as much justification, against Cobden and the Manchester School, whose teaching provided the inspiration for the thinking of Roosevelt's Secretary of State, Cordell Hull. But like Cobden, Hull and colleagues could see no incompatibility between the welfare of their own countrymen and that of everyone else. It was, after all, fundamental to the liberal creed that there was no necessary conflict of interests among the diverse nations of the world. Neither commerce nor politics were zero-sum games, and what was good for Manchester, or Detroit, was almost by definition good for mankind.

The converse of this amiable creed, unfortunately, was that if this hidden hand of Providence did not operate, it must be the fault of either ignorance or of interested malice on the part of those concerned. Confronted by disagreement, by an apparently flat incompatibility of interests and views, it was all too easy to pass from reasoned argument

---

3   Robert Divine, *Second Chance: the Triumph of Internationalism in World War II* (New Jersey 1967), pp. 70, 73.
4   Especially Gabriel Kolko, *The Politics of War: Allied Diplomacy and the World Crisis of 1943–5* (London 1969).

through puzzled exasperation to denunciation of one's adversary as being, in some cosmic sense, malevolent, dangerous and wrong; and this of course was to happen with tragic rapidity after the war in the relationship between the United States and the Soviet Union.

But during the war it was not the Soviet Union which was seen in Washington as being likely to cause the greatest difficulties after the war. Russia was a largely unknown quantity from which everyone, especially President Roosevelt, hoped for the best, and whose bitterest critics were at least temporarily silenced by the victories of the Red Army. The real obstacle to the implementation of the new world order was seen by many American liberals to lie in Britain, with her economic zone of imperial preference, with her sterling area, with her Machiavellian skill at power politics, with her colonial empire holding millions of the coloured races in subjection, with her smooth, accomplished diplomats and well-prepared staff-officers once again ensnaring the unwary Americans in the old game of secret diplomacy and the balance of power.[5]

Now it is perfectly true that the British Government did not share the sanguine expectations of American liberals about the nature of the post-war world: it had a more lively and realistic insight into the political and above all the economic difficulties which were likely to confront the Allies after their victory. The Foreign Office documents which are now becoming available do indeed reveal a traditionalism in British thinking about the post-war world; but the tradition was that, not of the balance of power, but of the Concert of Europe—not that of Pitt, but that of Castlereagh. British officials stressed the need for the victorious powers to remain together at almost any cost in order to manage the post-war world in general and post-war Europe in particular. Above all, the United States had to be persuaded to abandon all thought of returning to her pre-war isolation, and if her price was an international organisation strongly weighted against colonialism, and an economic order strongly weighted against eco-

---

[5] For American military suspicions of British intentions see Albert C. Wedemeyer, *Wedemeyer Reports* (New York 1958). For suspicions of Britain's nuclear intentions, see M.M. Gowing, *Britain and Atomic Energy, 1939–1945* (London 1964). For economic difficulties, see Richard N. Gardner, *Sterling-Dollar Diplomacy* (Oxford University Press 1956).

nomic preferences and tariff areas, that price had to paid. American withdrawal from an international system which the British now knew they could never have the strength to manage was seen in London as the ultimate disaster. But almost as bad, in the eyes of the Foreign Office, was the prospect of the settled and implacable hostility of the Soviet Union; for if the Soviet Union were to fall out with its Western Allies, a situation would arise which Germany would not fail to exploit, and use, as France had exploited Allied divisions after 1815, to re-establish herself as a Great Power.[6]

It would be a rash man, in the absence of adequate documentation, who attempted a definitive account of Russian aims and motives in 1945; but fortunately many rash men have done so, and one can now make statements about them which, although far from authoritative, are something more than speculation.[7] The policy of the Soviet Union, or rather of Joseph Stalin, appears to have been based even more squarely on traditional principles of power politics than was even that of the United Kingdom. Stalin's main nightmare, like that of the British, was probably the revival of German power; but he saw little prospect of dealing with this simply by co-operating with bourgeois States whose fundamental hostility to the Soviet Union he saw no cause to question. In a world with no certain allies it was clearly wise to extend one's frontiers by unilateral action and consolidate one's power as far to the west as possible; certainly as far as the frontiers of the Russian Empire as they had existed before the Treaty of Brest Litovsk.

Stalin had made his intentions clear to the British as early as December 1941; and embarrassing as they were to the nation whose guarantee to uphold the integrity and independence of Poland had brought them into the war in the first place, the British realised that there was little they could do about them. In the division of Eastern Europe into 'spheres of influence' which Stalin and Churchill, in one of the most blatant acts of old-style *realpolitik* since the French Rev-

---

6   British official thinking can be traced in the records of the Post-Hostilities Planning Committee for 1943–45 in the Public Records Office, CAB 81.
7   Of the numerous works by American and British sovietologists I would single out Adam B. Ulam, *Expansion and Co-Existence; the History of Soviet Foreign Policy 1917–1967* (London 1968) as the most persuasive.

olution, had made in the autumn of 1944, the British laid no claim to influence in Poland at all. But for the United States the situation was intolerable. It was made so not simply by the problem of the ethnic vote at home, as Roosevelt explained to an apparently sympathetic Stalin at Tehran. The *principle* was all important. 'I am afraid,'[8] Averill Harriman, American Ambassador in Moscow, explained to President Truman in June 1945, 'that Stalin does not and never will understand our interest in a free Poland as a matter of principle. He is a realist in all his actions and it is hard for him to appreciate our faith in abstract principles.'

Others in the United States made less effort to understand the Soviet attitude. Had not Stalin signed the Declaration on Liberated Europe at Yalta, thereby promising to assist the Poles 'to form interim governmental authorities broadly representative of all democratic elements in the population and pledged to the earliest possible establishment through free elections of governments responsive to the will of the people'?[9] And was he not in breach of this pledge, not only in Poland but in Romania and in every other country in Eastern Europe controlled by the Red Army? And was not the Red Army followed by an apparatus of totalitarian repression which bore a disquieting resemblance to that of the German occupation from which these lands had only just been liberated? Had the war been fought and American blood shed simply to substitute one tyranny for another?

American officials like Harriman and his deputy in Moscow, George Kennan, saw the problem in more moderate, more old-fashioned terms—terms not of justice but of power. Soviet power, as Kennan pointed out in his famous cable of February 1946,[10] was naturally expanding in the wake of Soviet armed strength; and in view of the deep suspicions which Soviet leaders harboured of the intentions of the bourgeois world, it would continue to expand un-

---

8   E.L. Gaddes, *The United States and the Origins of the Cold War 1941–47* (New York 1972), p. 234.

9   See above, p. 114.

10 Printed as Appendix C of George Kennan, *Memoirs 1925–1950* (London & New York 1963).

til it received a check. Soviet power must therefore be contained, by firm declarations of interest and, where necessary, by displays of strength; by operating in fact, the traditional mechanism of the balance of power. Poland might have to be yielded, but there were other areas as yet unconquered where Soviet expansion seemed to threaten: the Mediterranean, for example.

In the Mediterranean the British found themselves engaged at the end of the war in a regional power confrontation whose origins went back to the early nineteenth century and which, under the harmless-sounding title of 'The Eastern Question' had been accepted by European statesmen almost as an intrinsic element in the pattern of power politics: the attempt, by supporting local governments in those regions, to prevent the Russians from establishing an ascendancy in the Middle East and the Levant. Britain's instruments in this confrontation were the governments of Greece and Turkey. The Western orientation of both was maintained by the traditional mechanisms of diplomatic pressure, financial aid and military support. But in February 1947 the British Government, in the grip of the first great economic crisis to affect it after the war, decided that the confrontation was too expensive to sustain. Subsidies to these two client states had come to an end. 'The Great Game' against Russia in the Mediterranean, which Stratford de Redcliffe had initiated a hundred years earlier, had to be abandoned.

Historians agree that it was this decision that compelled the United States Government to make its first clear and overt move in the field of European power politics; but it could not be presented as such to a Congress congenitally suspicious of picking British imperial chestnuts out of the fire. The Republican leaders made it clear to the Administration that they could support such a move if it were explained in terms that would make sense to the liberal conscience;[11] and in consequence President Truman clothed what old-style European statesmen would have seen as a disagreeable but necessary local commitment within a traditional system of power-balances, in all the panoply of a call to arms in a Manichean confrontation against the forces of darkness:

---

11 Dean Acheson, *Present at the Creation* (New York 1969), p. 219.

Our way of life [Truman declared in March 1947] is based upon the will of the majority, and is distinguished by free institutions, representative governments, free election, guarantees of individual liberty, freedom of speech and religion and freedom from political oppression. The *second* way of life is based upon the will of a minority forcibly imposed on the majority. It relies upon terror and oppression, a controlled press and radio, fixed elections and the suppression of personal freedoms. [The United States, said Truman, would] not realise our objectives unless we are willing to help free peoples to maintain their institutions and their national integrity against aggressive movements that seek to impose on them totalitarian *régimes*. [As a result the United States had to] support free peoples who are resisting attempted subjugation by armed minorities or by outside pressures ... The free peoples *of the world* [my italics] look to us for support in maintaining their freedoms. If we falter in our leadership we may endanger the peace of the world.[12]

Such was the Truman doctrine.

So now the American people knew where they stood—in the front line of that confrontation between the forces of democracy and the forces of totalitarianism, the forces of freedom and the forces of tyranny, from which they had stood so disastrously aside when it had first developed in Europe ten years earlier. They were not going to make that mistake again. Nor were they going to make the mistake of 'appeasing' the enemy. As the Republican senator Vandenberg put it, to quote only one voice in a mighty chorus, 'Appeasement simply feeds the hazard from which it seeks to escape ... Munich was a ghastly mistake.'[13] This time the United States would stand firm against the aggression which, in 1948, seemed about to unroll; in Czecho-Slovakia in February 1948, a melancholy decade after its first rape; in Berlin in June of the same year, where the Soviet-imposed blockade, which was probably a local manoeuvre in the complex framework of Allied disagreement over occupation policy, was magnified by the harassed American commander in Germany into a deliberate attempt to test the nerve of the entire Free World, and so evoked an appropriately heroic response;[14] and above all two years

---

12 Harry S. Truman, *Memoirs*, vol. II. Years of Trial and Hope 1946–53 (London 1956), p. 112.

13 Wheeler Bennett & Nicholls, op. cit. p. 431.

14 J.E. Smith, ed. *The Papers of General Lucius D. Clay* (Bloomington and London 1974), vol. II, esp. pp. 447–623.

later in Korea, where the North Korean attack in June 1950 seemed to give proof that the Communist threat was world wide. Here the lessons of the Thirties appeared at their least equivocal. President Truman had recorded his own reaction to the news of the North Korean attack:[15]

> In my generation, this was not the first time that the strong had attacked the weak. I recalled some earlier instances, Manchuria, Ethiopia, Austria. I remembered how, each time the democracies failed to act, it had encouraged the aggressors to keep going ahead ... If the Communists were permitted to force their way into the Republic of Korea without opposition from the Free World, no small nation would have the courage to resist threats and aggression by stronger communist neighbours.

So this time collective security must be made to work, and thanks to the American leadership and fortuitous Soviet absence from the United Nations at the crucial moment, work it did—for the first and so far the last time. America and her associates went to the aid of South Korea flying the flag of the United Nations, fulfilling their obligations under the Charter as, only fifteen years earlier, the members of the League of Nations should have gone to the aid of Abyssinia but disastrously did not. They were the *posse comitatus,* enforcing the rule of law against the malefactors and their associates; in particular the People's Republic of China which, by helping the North Koreans, brought aid and comfort to the aggressors and so disqualified itself as a peace-loving power worthy of admission to the United Nations. The American liberal conscience, and that of their European and other associates, was quite clear: this also was a profoundly just war. If similar action had been taken fifteen years earlier, the Second World War—what Winston Churchill had called the 'unnecessary war'—might never have had to be fought.

The result of the Korean War was quite simply to militarise the United States. In some respects indeed it appeared almost providential. Even those members of the American administration who adopted the most moderate views of 'containment' had agreed that the task would call for the creation of a peacetime 'defence establishment' on a scale beyond precedent in American history; and up till

---

15 Truman, op. cit. p. 351.

June 1950 there was little sign that the American people, whatever their noble intentions, were prepared to pay the price of being a world power.[16] Korea changed all that. Defence appropriations were quadrupled almost overnight and continued to soar. The Republicans in Congress attacked the Truman Administration, not for doing too much, but for not doing enough and for not having done it earlier. The moderates in the State Department who refused to see the conflict in Manichean terms, even that hardened power-politician Dean Acheson, were accused of being 'soft on Communism' if not indeed covert members of the Communist Party. If this was indeed a just war, then it was a crusade in which there could be no compromise, no substitute for victory. The Republican Party in the Presidential Elections of 1952 promised that:

> we shall again make liberty into a beacon-light of hope that will penetrate the dark places. It will mark the end of the negative, futile and immoral policy of 'containment' which abandons countless human beings to a despotism and godless terrorism which in turn enables their rulers to forge the captives into a weapon for our destruction ... The policies we espouse will revive the contagious, liberating influences which are inherent in freedom.[17]

It is not likely that this rhetoric was any more effective in bringing the Republicans to power than were the simultaneous and contradictory promises by the Presidential candidate, General Eisenhower, that he would end the now stalemated and expensive war in Korea and restore financial normalcy. But the managers of the Republican Party would hardly have used such language if they had not good reason to suppose that it would pay political dividends, and although Eisenhower's own foreign policy was in fact to be rather more cautious and pragmatic than that of his predecessor, the rhetoric continued to flow unabated from the capacious mouth of his Secretary of State, John Foster Dulles. When in January 1957 the Administration sought Congressional approval for military moves which might become necessary in the Middle East to shore up the Western posi-

---

16 Paul Y. Hammond, 'NSC-68: Prologue to Rearmament' in Warner R. Schilling and others, *Strategy, Policy and Defence Budgets* (New York and London 1962), pp. 267-379.
17 Quoted in T. Hoopes, *The Devil & John Foster Dulles* (London 1974), p. 130.

tion after the catastrophic Suez affair, this had to be presented as the use of US armed forces to defend Middle East nations 'against overt armed aggression from any nation controlled by international communism'; so the Eisenhower Doctrine was added to the Truman Doctrine as a pledge of commitment in cold but total war. But as Paul Hammond has put it, in his succinct and perceptive study of American foreign policy:

> Had [Eisenhower] articulated and publicised his inclination to moderate the arms race and be conciliatory to the Russians, he would probably have paid a significant political price in domestic popularity, effectiveness and public trust.[18]

The American liberal conscience of the fifties, tutored by its European mentors of the Thirties, could understand and support either a just war or perpetual peace, and it appreciated that the former might be necessary to achieve the latter. It had no time for any shifts and manoeuvres, any deals or compromises, that might lie between the two.

The men both of the Truman and the Eisenhower administrations knew this very well. Many of them appreciated the exaggerated and rhetorical nature of their declaratory policy. But to confront and contain Soviet power, even in the most limited *realpolitik* situations, they needed power of their own, and if popular constraints presented them with the sole alternatives of impotence and overkill, they settled for the latter—and, with it, for the greatest arms race in the history if the world.

Yet the difference between the expert perceptions and popular rhetoric was not always very great. Nowhere was it narrower than in the case of Vietnam. In November 1951 Dean Rusk, then Assistant Secretary of State for Far Eastern Affairs, made a speech setting out official American policy towards, as it then was, French Indo-China:

> The real issue in Indo-China is whether the peoples of that land will be permitted to work out their future as they see fit, or whether they will be subjected to a Communist reign of terror and be absorbed by force into the new colonialism of a Soviet Communist Empire. In this situation it is generally agreed in the United States that we should support and assist the

---

18 Paul Y. Hammond, *The Cold War Years: American Foreign Policy since 1945* (New York 1969), p. 136.

armies of France and of the associated States in meeting the armed threat in Indo-China.[19]

So the Truman Doctrine was extended to Vietnam, and the French armies and their supporters were cast in the role of 'free peoples resisting attempted subjugation'. But the confidential calculations of *realpolitik* in the National Security Council presented a more alarming picture:

The loss of any of the countries of South East Asia to communist control [ran one report in June 1952] as a consequence of overt or covert Chinese Communist aggression would have critical psychological, political and economic consequences. In the absence of effective and timely counteraction, the loss of any single country would probably lead to relatively swift submission to or alignment with Communism by the remaining countries of this group. Furthermore an alignment with Communism of the rest of South East Asia and India, and in the longer term of the Middle East ... would in all probability follow...[20]

And eighteen months later in January 1954 a further confidential report was even more disturbing:

In the conflict in Indo-China, the Communist and non-Communist worlds clearly confront one another on the field of battle: the loss of the struggle in Indo-China, in addition to its impact in South-East Asia and South Asia, would therefore have the most serious repercussions in US and free-world interests in Europe and elsewhere.[21]

Vietnam in short was depicted as the hole in the dike which held back the floodwaters of Communism from submerging the Free World. Thanks to his own caution and that of his European allies, President Eisenhower was able to resist the advice of his officials, that he should select it as the battleground where the fortunes of democracy were to be put to the test. Ten years later, in 1964, his successor was not to be so restrained.

One can see the implications of these perceptions only too clearly. In the first place, the adversary was dehumanised. He ceased to be

---

19 Quoted in David Halberstam, *The Best and the Brightest* (New York 1969), p. 330.
20 *The Pentagon Papers*, Gravel Edition (Boston 1971), vol. I, p. 83.
21 Ibid. p. 434.

a party with fears, perceptions, interests and difficulties of his own; one with whom rational discussion and compromise was possible. Any move made by the Soviet Union was interpreted as a gambit in a settled scheme of world conquest. Any opposition from any quarter to United States power traced back to the manipulations of Moscow; and 'world communism' was seen as a single monolithic, subtle, patient and powerful adversary, Apollyon and Lucifer combined, if not indeed the Beast in the Book of Revelations which made war against the Saints and prevailed against them.

Secondly, every State and every regime whose interests coincided with those of the United States automatically became part of the 'Free World', honorary democracies whatever the nature of their political system. The criterion of 'freedom' rapidly ceased to be that defined by Truman: 'Free institutions, representative governments, free elections, guarantees of individual liberty, freedom of speech and religion and freedom from political oppression.' It became, rather, accessibility to American influence and willingness to fall in with the wishes of the United States.

And finally, those who made trouble for America's allies—liberation movements in colonies, socialist or liberal opposition to friendly dictatorships, even dissident tribal movements of long standing—all tended to be seen as clients of Moscow; an attitude which proved all too often a self-fulfilling prophecy. Nationalist movements and self-proclaimed 'wars of national liberation' which, under a top dressing of revolutionary rhetoric, unconsciously owed more to the political and military teaching of Mazzini than they did to that of Marx and Lenin, movements such as in Italy and the Balkans in the nineteenth century liberals had approved and supported, were now seen as subtle manoeuvres whereby world communism was undermining and subverting the Free World.

By the 1960s many liberals in the United States were growing uneasy about the situation. The vast military establishment with its industrial ramifications and its horrific weapons-systems, the dubious allies shored up by arms and dollars; the blind hostility to two vast states containing between them half the population of the world—was all this really necessary to defend the democratic way of life? The traditional pacifist and isolationist elements in American society protested with increasing vehemence. The traditional internationalists agitated for disarmament and a relaxation of international tensions. The traditional radicals denounced the new 'military-industrial complex'. A new generation defiantly took the leaders of the liberation movements—Castro, Che Guevera—as their heroes and saw in the 'freedom fighters' a life-style which they attempted to recreate at home.

The war in Vietnam, by forcing the American government to back its rhetoric by action, brought matters to a head. It revealed what a hideous gap separated rhetoric from reality. Whatever was being defended in South Vietnam, it was not democracy as Americans understood it. Whatever the potential evils the war was being fought to avert, the actual evils it was inflicting on the Vietnamese people themselves were starkly depicted on every television screen. Whatever the ideology of the Vietnamese insurgents, they were obviously fighting with dedicated skill and heroism. Whatever support they might be getting from Peking or Moscow, the North Vietnamese and the Vietcong were clearly no passive tools of 'international communism'. And the appalling suspicion began to grow among American liberals that the United States, the very embodiment of democratic and peaceful values, might, as it approached the end of its second century, be waging a murderously oppressive war against a small people struggling to be free.

It would not be relevant to our subject to dwell on the irony of America's rescue from her predicament by a European-born admirer of Metternich, Dr Henry Kissinger: a man whose name was to become synonymous with power politics, secret diplomacy, and all the apparatus of international manoeuvre which American liberals hoped they had put behind them forever. Kissinger set himself the astonishing task of transforming the Manichean confrontation of the past thirty years into a global equivalent of the Old Concert of Europe, wherein the Great Powers would collaborate in preserving the framework of an orderly international system which would enable them to pursue their own interests within tacitly accepted limits imposed by the generally accepted need to avoid dangerous confrontation: a system within which the military power of the adversary was recognised and accepted as an essential and legitimate element in the maintenance of international stability. American liberals watched this process with a kind of stunned bewilderment, but since it was so self-evidently preferable to what had gone before they made only muted protests; except when, in a particularly brutal exhibition of *Machtpolitik*, Kissinger extended the conflict to Cambodia. Only now is President Carter reasserting more traditional American values in foreign policy. Whether he will succeed in creating a synthesis between the universalist liberal values which he professes and the framework of power politics which he has inherited yet remains to be seen.

What conclusions are we to draw form this melancholy story of the efforts of good men to abolish war but only succeeding thereby in making it more terrible? Let us look again at some of the beliefs which they have professed.

First there was the view which underlay the writings of Erasmus, which was expounded at the beginning of the seventeenth century by Crucé, and which became the orthodoxy both of the eighteenth-century *philosophes* and of the nineteenth-century Cobdenites: that wars occurred because they were a way of life among a militarised aristocratic ruling class and would die out when this was replaced by what St. Simon called *les industrieux*. The inadequacy of such an explanation was proved by events. The disappearance of the aristocracy was accompanied by an intensification, not a diminution of warfare. What can perhaps be said is that it was because of the social structure of Europe from the seventeenth to the nineteenth centuries, because of the dominance of an aristocratic warrior elite, that wars took the form that they then did; that they occurred so frequently but also that they were so limited in their scope.

The transition to democracy, as Clausewitz was the first thinker to recognise, so far from abolishing war, brought into it an entirely new dimension of violent passion to which advances in technology could, unfortunately, give full reign. Democracies, from France at the end of the eighteenth century to the United States in the middle of the twentieth, have failed to live up to the expectations of the eighteenth-century liberal thinkers. On the contrary they have repeatedly displayed bellicose passion reminiscent of the worst years of the Wars of Religion. They may in general, as Tocqueville rightly discerned, be uninterested in foreign affairs, hostile to alliances and sceptical about such abstract concepts as the balance of power. On the other hand their ignorance of foreign politics makes them suspicious and xenophobe, prone to paranoia, and passionately vindictive in proportion to the shattering of their peaceful ideals. Moreover, the liberal theory took no account of totalitarianism; the extent to which an entire society can be held captive by ideologues who, by manipulating all forms of communication, can either inculcate a positively militaristic philosophy as did the Fascists or, in a hermetically sealed society such as the Soviet Union and the People's Republic of China, teach successive generations to believe as a matter of faith in the unremitting hostility of the outside world. The doctrine that peoples if left to themselves are *naturally* peaceable, like its converse that they are *naturally* belligerent, begs far more questions than it answers.

Secondly, there was the associated belief which came into prominence in the nineteenth century: that wars resulted not from aristocratic habit but from the vested interests and distorted perceptions of a governing class and the capitalist interests— particularly those of armaments manufacturers—which it represented. Certainly armaments races exacerbate international tensions, but they are as much the consequences of those tensions as the cause. The relationship is at best symbiotic. As for the clash of capitalist interests, few historians would today see this as a major factor in the origins of either world war. In particular, the part played by imperial rivalries in both was minimal. In both, indeed, the British found more hostility to their imperial interests among their allies than they did among their enemies.

Thirdly, liberals laid the blame for war on the diplomats and their manipulation of the balance of power. Again, clumsy diplomacy and ruthless power politics can cause wars, much as bad driving can cause traffic accidents. But power politics, as Norman Angell came to recognise, are the politics of not being overpowered. All the liberal thinkers we have considered, with the exceptions only of Erasmus and Jonathan Dymond, were prepared to fight wars of self-defence. But it is the business of statesmen and diplomats to make it unnecessary to fight such wars or to ensure that, if they do come, their country should not be confronted by a coalition so overwhelming, and be left so bereft of help, that it fights in a helpless cause. To transcend this necessity and create a genuine world system of collective security has been the aim of liberal statesmen throughout this century. But such a system demands a degree of mutual confidence, a homogeneity of values and a coincidence of perceived interests such as did not exist even in the limited society of inter-war Europe. We are a long way from creating it in the culturally heterogeneous world which we inhabit today.

The basic fact that has been recognised by every serious political thinker who has turned his attention to the matter—by More and Bacon, by Hobbes and Locke, by Montesquieu and Rousseau, by Kant and Hegel—is that war is an inherent element in a system of sovereign states which lacks any supreme and acknowledged arbiter; and the more genuinely those states, by reason of their democratic structure, embody indigenous and peculiar cultural values and perceptions, the less likely are they to sacrifice that element of sovereignty which carries with it the decision if necessary to use force to protect their interests. The answer cannot lie, as Rousseau sardonically suggested, in the dissolution of the sovereign state for, as Rousseau also perceived, it is only by the creation of a sovereign state with which they can completely identify themselves that men can feel themselves to be fully free. To this extent surely Mazzini was right: in order to have internationalism one must first create nations; and those peoples who have already achieved cultural self-consciousness and political independence can all too easily forget the claims of those who have not. In the era of the French revolution French liberals ignored German nationalism. In 1848 the German liberals ignored Slav nationalism.[22] In the era of the First World War Western liberals were increasingly embarrassed by the claims of East European nationalism. And since the Second World War liberals of Western

---

22 It is interesting to compare Fichte's attack on the egocentricity of French Nationalism in his Thirteenth Address to the German Nation (Sämmtiche Werke, (Leipzig 1845–6) vol. viii, pp. 459–80) with the way the German liberals at the Frankfurt Assembly in 1848 treated 'the attempts of puny nationalities to found their own lives in our midst, and like parasites to destroy ours.' (L.B. Namier, *1848: the Revolution of the Intellectuals*, p. 120.)

Europe and the United States have only slowly and painfully come to terms with the nationalism of the Third World. Frantz Fanon was saying no more than Mazzini had before him when he maintained that there are times when the only way of asserting an identity may be by the use of force.[23] Where Mazzini and imitators were at fault was in assuming that because the creation of nation states was a necessary condition for peace, it would also be a sufficient one.

At the root of this dilemma of liberal thinkers lies the habit, far older even than Erasmus, of seeing war as a distinct and abstract entity about which one can generalise at large. It was this habit of thought that made possible the ludicrous confusion of the interwar years when liberals declared themselves passionately opposed to 'war' but in favour of 'military sanctions' to enforce collective security or, even more strongly, in favour of 'resistance to Fascism'. It has made it possible for enthusiasts in our own day to declare their opposition to war but their support for struggles for national liberation. But 'war' is simply the generic term for the use of armed force by states or aspirants to statehood for the attainment of their political objectives. One may support the use of force to attain certain objectives but not others. One may support the use of force by some actors in the international system but not by others. One may support the use of certain kinds of force but not others. Only those absolute pacifists who, like Gandhi, totally renounce the use of force to defend themselves or their societies can claim to be opposed to war. And if they do so renounce the use of force while others do not, then not only their own survival but that of their value-system can be at a very high risk.

This does not mean that the liberal tradition in thinking about war and peace has been totally self-deluding and false. It has certainly been a tradition often marred by naiveté, by intellectual arrogance, by ignorance, by confused thinking and sometimes, alas, by sheer hypocrisy. But how can one fail to share the aspirations of those who carried on this tradition, or deny credit to their achievements? It is thanks to the patient work, over nearly two centuries, of the men and women who have been inspired by the liberal conscience that so much progress has been made in the creation of a global

---

23   Frantz Fanon, *The Wretched of the Earth* (London 1965).

community of nations; that values are today asserted as universal to which all states, virtually without exception, pay at least lip-service; that it is recognised, even if only in principle, that states have communal obligations and duties within a freely-accepted framework of international society. The danger lies in forgetting that each actor in this society of states, including those who have not yet achieved statehood, embodies distinct cultural perceptions and values; that it is ultimately concerned quite inevitably and properly with its own survival; and that it is unwilling, whatever declarations may be made to the contrary, totally to rely on the power and will of the international community as a whole to protect it.

We have thus not yet escaped from the world of power politics and *raison d'état*. Nor does an increasing multiplicity of national actors in itself guarantee a more peaceful and a better-ordered world. Kant was right when he said that a state of peace had to be 'established'. What perhaps even he did discern was that this is a task which has to be tackled afresh every day of our lives; and that no formula, no organisation and no political or social revolution can ever free mankind from this inexorable duty.

INDEX

Abyssinia, 79, 80-2, 88
Acheson, Dean, 110
Adams, John, 19
Adler, Victor, 59, 72
Alabama, 44
Alexander, Prince of Scotland, 6
Allen, Clifford, 91-93
Allen, William, 32
Angell, Norman, 50, 60, 65, 68, 73, 83, 94
appeasement, 90, 92, 93, 94, 108
arbitration, 11, 44, 66, 75
Argenson, Marquis d', 16
aristocracy, 12, 15, 19, 34, 53, 115
armaments, disarmament: arms races, 116; pre-1914, 52, 54-5, 65-6, 70; since 1945, 111; Bentham on, 25; Labour Party and, 86-7; League of Nations and, 75
Atlantic Charter, 99, 103
Attlee, Clement, 79, 81-2, 86, 87, 97

Bacon, Francis, 12
balance of power; Bright and Cobden, 34-5; Britain and Fascism, 81-2, 85-6, 94; First World War, 35, 61, 64; Gladstone, 46; Morel, 65; *see also* Concert of Europe; diplomacy

Balkan League, 50
Bastiat, Frédéric, 30
Bebel, Agust, 57, 61
Belgium, German invasion of, 63
Bell, Julian, 89-90
Betham, Jeremy, 24-7
Bevan Aneurin, 3, 94, 96
Bevin Ernest, 78
Boer War, 2, 58
Boulanger, General, 52
bourgeoisie (middle classes, q.v.), 52-3
Brailsford, H.N., 48, 50, 56(2), 57, 60-1, 68-9, 74
Bright. John, 2, 33-7, 47, 56n.
Britain: basis of foreign policy of, 25; and France, 25, 59; and Germany, 52, 63-4, 67-9, 73-4, 85, 90-7; and League of Nations, 78-82, 85; and the Middle East, 46-8, 107, 110-1; public schools in, 5; and the Soviet Union, 105-6, 107-8; and the USA, 99-100, 104-5, 107
Bryce, Lord, 66
Buxton, Noel, 73

capitalism, 53, 59-60, 61, 77-8, 116
Carnegie, Andrew, 69-70

Carter, President, 115
Castiglione, Baldassare, 7
Cecil, Viscount, 75, 76
Chamberlain, Joseph, 51
Chamberlain, Neville, 95
Christianity, Christian Church, 5, 8, 30
Churchill, Winston, 94, 105, 109
Civil War, American, 43
Clausewitz, Karl von, 115
Clemenceau, Georges, 72
Cobbett, William, 23, 35
Cobden, Richard, 32-7, 41, 45, 56n., 103
Colbert, Jean Baptiste, 15-16
collective security, 75, 78-80, 82, 84-8, 109, 117; *see also* Concert of Europe; League of Nations; United Nations
colonies, colonial rivalry, *see* imperialism
commerce, *see* trade
communism, 111-5; *see also* Communist Party, British; Marx; Soviet Union
Communist Party, British, 94-5, 96
Comte, Auguste, 30
Concert of Europe, public law of; Europe/of nations, 13, 46, 47, 48, 64, 76, 94, 98, 104; *see also* balance of power; collective security
Condorcet, Marquis de, 19
conscientious objection, 89-90, 91
courts, international, 25, 47; *see also* arbitration
Crimean War, 32, 36
Cripps, Sir Stafford, 3, 77, 79, 83, 95
Crucé, Eméric, 10-12, 115
cultures, not homogenous, 26-7, 72
Czechoslovakia, 73, 92, 94, 108

Daily Herald, 85
Daily News, 64

Dalton, Hugh, 85
democracy, 27, 37, 67, 69-72, 89, 97, 99, 108, 112, 114, 115; *see also* 'people, the'; Union for Democratic Control
Déroulède, Paul, 51
Dickinson, Goldsworthy Lowes, 68-73
diplomacy, secret diplomacy, 19, 25, 56, 85; *see also* balance of power; Concert of Europe; treaties
disarmament, *see* armaments
Dittman, Wilhelm, 59
Dreyfus Affair, 52
Dulles, John Foster, 110
Dymond, Jonathan, 31, 116

Eastern Question, *see* Middle East
economic development, *see* trade
Eden, Sir Anthony, 47
Egypt, 47; Suez crisis, 47, 111
Eisenhower, Dwight D., 110-12
Endowment for International Peace, 70, 71
England, *see* Britain
Erasmus, Desiderius, 5-8, 11, 12, 15, 18, 115, 116, 118

Fanon, Frantz, 118
Fascism, 83-100 (sp. 88-9), 115; *see also* Abyssinia
Fichte, Johann Gottlieb, 39
First World War, Great War, 3, 59-62, 63-5, 69-73
Fischer, Fritz, 52
Fox, Charles James, 36
Fox, George, 30
France: eighteenth century, 14-16 20-1; Napoleonic Wars, 21, 22, 27-8, 31; nineteenth century, 25, 51-2
Free Trade Movement, 32-35; *see also* trade
freedom; national, *see* nationalism

INDEX

Fried, Alfred, 55

Gandhi, Mohandes, 118
Gardiner, A.G., 64
Garibaldi, Gieuseppe, 2, 42
Germany: and Britain, 52, 81, 85-6, 90-1, 94-8; grievances of, after Versailles, 91-4; militarism, military power of, 51, 67-8, 81, 85-6, 94-7, 105(2); national feeling in, 39; reform of, projected, 71-2, 95-9; tricolour flag of, 24
Gilbert, Dr Felix, 102
Gladstone, William Ewart, 45-7
Goudar, Ange, 16
Green, T.H., 49
Grey, Sir Edward, 55, 63-4
Grotius, Hugo, 10, 11

Hague Conferences, 44
Hammond, Paul, 111
Hankey, Sir Maurice, 80-82
Harriman, Averell, 106
Herder, Johann Gottfried von, 39
Hervé, Gustav, 57
'hidden hand', providence, 12, 17, 45, 49, 103-4
Hitler, Adolf, 85
Hoare, Sir Samuel, 81-2, 81n.
Hobbes, Thomas, 12, 14
Hobhouse, L.T., 49-50, 58
Hobson, J.A., 48, 53-4, 73, 74, 91-2
Hull, Cordell, 98, 103

imperialism, colonial rivalry, 25, 53-4, 77, 91-2
Independent Labour Party, 73
'industrieux, les', producing classes, 29-30, 51, 115
Inter-Parliamentary Union, 44
International, Socialist; 56, 61; *see also* socialism

internationalism; 2-3, 25-6, 51, 84, 117; *see also* collective security; Concert of Europe; League of Nations; United Nations
interventionism; 68; *see also* collective security; non-intervention
Italy, liberation of, 40 (*see also* Garibaldi; Mazzini); *see also* Abyssinia

Juarés, Jean, 56, 57

Kant, Immanuel, 16-18, 119
Kautsky, Karl, 61
Kennan, George, 106-7
kings, monarchs, 16-17, 18, *see also* ruling classes
Kissinger, Dr Henry, 114-15
Korean War, 85, 109-10

Labour Party, 73, 75, 77-9, 83, 85-8, 91, 93, 97
Lansbury, George, 77, 79
Laski, Harold, 77, 83
League to Enforce Peace, 66, 75
League of Nations, 66, 74-80, 85
League of Nations Society, 66
League of Nations Union, 75
Liberalism, liberal conscience, 3, 115-19; and Abyssinian War, 82; dilemma posed by the uncivilised, 44-5; eighteenth-century mainstream of liberal thinking, 14, 23-4; and First World War, 63-5; and Germany, in 1945, 96-7; Gladstone, 45-8; nternational community, 47-8, 84, 101; *see also* internationalism, middle-class character of liberalism, 56; militarism opposed by, 64; and the Second World War, 93-5, 101-2; Trevelyan, 1; in USA, 101-2, 107-8, 111; and Versailles, 72-3;

Woodrow Wilson's programme, 71
liberation movements, *see* national liberation movements
Ligue Internationale de la Paix et de la Liberté, 41-2
List, Friedrich, 39-40
Lloyd, George, David, 50, 72
Locke, John, 12
Lothian, Philip, 91

McCulloch, John, 28-9
MacDonald, James Ramsay, 59, 65
Machiavelli, Niccoló, 8
Manchester Guardian, 33, 64
Martin, Kingsley; 85, 89, 90, 92, 93, 95; *see also New Statesman*
Martin, Laurence, 70
Marx, Marxism, 16, 53, 54
masses, the, *see* 'people, the'
Mazzini, Giuseppe, 26, 37-8, 40, 117-18
Mediterranean area, *see* Middle East
Melon, Jean-François, 16
middle classes, 27-8, 51-3, 56
Middle East; *see also* Egypt; Turks
Mill, James, 28
Mill, John Stuart, 29, 41, 45
Milner, Alfred, 51
monarchy, monarchs, *see* kings Motesquieu, Charles de Secondat, Baron de, 12-13, 16
More, Thomas, 8-10
Morel, E.D., 55-6, 65-6, 74
Moscow Declaration, 99
Muir, Ramsay, 74
Murray, Gilbert, 74

Namier, L.B., 69
Napoleonic Wars, 27, 28, 31, 38-9
national liberation movements, present day, 24, 113, 118

nationalism, nations, self-determination: Atlantic Charter, 99; and Fascism, 83, 94-5; First World War, 61-2, 63, 72-3; in France, 38-9; in Germany, 39-40, 92; internationalism dependent on, 117-18; Mazzini, 37-8, 40, 117, 118; nineteenth-century view of, 24; Peace Movement and, 38, 41; small nations, 49-50, 68, 94; Spain, 89-90; USA and, 99-100, 107-8, 113
Nazis, Nazism, 91, 95-6
New Stateman; 86, 92, 93, 95 *see also* Martin Kingsley
non-intervention, 35-6; *see also* interventionism

Orlando, Vittorio Emanuele, 72
Ottoman Empire, *see* Turks
Oxford Union, 80

pacifism, pacifists, 26-7, 30-1, 77
Paine, Thomas, 20-1, 23, 24
Palmerston, Lord, 34
peace: basis of liberal thinking on, 24; Bentham on, 24-7; and democracy, 23, 72, 99, 115; established, has to be, 17-18, 119; and nationalism, 24, 82, 107-8, 117-18; and republics, 16-17, 19, 21; revolution to secure, 20, 21, 24, 83; and trade, commerce, *see* trade 'without victory', 81; *see also* war
Peace Ballot, 76-7, 84
Peace Convention, Peace Congresses, 32, 44
Peace Movement, Peace Societies, 27-42 (sp. 27, 32-3, 37-8, 41-2,) 43-4, 69-70, 90
Peace Pledge, 76n.
'people, the', public opinion, peaceful/bellicose nature of, 115-6;

Crimean War, 36; Fascism, 88-9; First World War, 59, 72; League of Nations, 76-7; liberals' definition of, 56; nineteenth-century view of, 24, 30, 84; working class, proletariat, masses, 56-9, 78; *see also* democracy
philosophes, 15, 24, 27, 115
Physiocrats, 16
Poincaré, M., 74
Poland, 94, 105, 106, 107
Pollitt, Harry, 88-9
Ponsonby, Arthur, 65, 73
press, freedom of, 26
producing classes, *see* 'industrieux, les'
proletariat, *see* 'people, the'
providence, workings of, *see* 'hidden hand'
public law of Europe, *see* Concert of Europe
public opinion, *see* 'people, the'
public schools, 51
Pufendorf, Samuel von, 10
Punch, 33

Quakers, Society of Friends, 30-1
Quesnay, François,

republics, peace and, 16-17, 19, 21
revolution, peace and, 20, 21, 24, 83
Richard, Henry, 41
Rights of Man, Declaration of, 39
Roosevelt, Franklin Delano, 100, 102, 103, 106
Rousseau, Jean-Jacques, 13-15, 18, 117
ruling classes, war as vested interest of: eighteenth-century view of, 15-20, 83, 115; Erasmus, 7; nineteenth-century view of, 34, 51-2, 115; socialist view of, 53, 77-8; *see also* warrior class
Rusk, Dean, 111-12

Russell, Bertrand, 67
Russia, *see* Soviet Union

Saint Pierre, Abbé, 13
Saint-Simon, Claude Henri, Comte de, 51, 52, 115
sanctions, 66, 76, 80-3, 85
Say, Jean-Baptiste, 29
Schleswig-Holstein, 34, 37, 43
Second World War, 95-100, 101, 109
secret diplomacy, *see* diplomacy
self-defence, 26-7, 33, 116
self-determination, *see* nationalism
Senior, Nassau, 41
Seton-Watson, R.W., 69
Shaw, George Bernard, 49, 58, 68, 77
small nations, *see under* nationalism
Smith, Adam, 12, 16
Snowden, Philip, 65
socialism, socialists, 24, 53, 56-9 *passim*, 61; *see also* Labour Party; Marx
Society of Friends, *see* Quakers Society for the Promotion of Permanent and Universal Peace, 32
Soviet Union, Russia, 104-7, 108-16
Spain, Spanish Civil War, 89-90, 93
Spender, Stephen, 89
Stalin, Joseph, 105-6
strike, against war, 57, 77-8
Suez crisis (1956), 47, 111

Taft, William Howard, 66
Taylor, A.J.P., 69, 101
Tocqueville, Alexis de, 115
Totalitarianism, 106, 108, 116; *see also* Fascism; Soviet Union trade, commerce, economic development: Bentham, 25; Britain, 25, 28, 32-4; Cobden and Bright, 32-4; Crucé, 11; eighteenth century, 16; List, 39-40; J.S. Mill, 29;

nineteenth century, 29-30, 32-4, 39; Paine, 20
Trades Union Congress, 87
treaties, to be public, 75; *see also* diplomacy
Trevelyan, Sir Charles, 1, 2-3, 65, 72-3, 77, 83
Trevelyan, George Macaulay, 1-2, 3, 34-5, 64
Truman, Harry S., 107-8, 109, 113
Turgot, Anne Robert Jacques, 16, 28
Turks, Ottoman Empire, 46, 50, 107

Ulam, Adam B., 105n.
Union for Democratic Control (UDC), 65, 67, 69, 70, 73, 96
United Nations Organisation, 100
United States of America: Civil War, 43; and First World War, 69-72; political character of, 19-20, 101-3; and Second World War, 97-100; since 1945, 103-5, 106-7, 108-115

Vandenberg, Senator, 108
Vattel, Eméric, 10
Veblen, Thorstein, 71-2
Versailles, Treaty of, 72-4, 75, 85, 93
Vietnam, 110-12, 114
Vliegen, 61

war: abolition of, 31 ; *see also* Peace Movement; and Christianity, 5, 8; and Colonialism, *see* imperialism and democracy; *see* democracy just: Erasmus, 7-8; Gladstone, 45-8; international community, 45-8, 66-70, 84, 101; Korea, 109; Middle Ages, 7-8, 9' militarism, to defeat, 64, 67; More, 8-9; nationalism, national liberation 24, 42, 51, 90, 95; Spain, 89-90; to end war, 89-90; medieval view of, 8, 9; misunderstanding as cause of, 11; and nationalism, *see* nationalism: natural, 17; necessary, 5, 10, 40, 45; not glorious, 6, 8; not natural, 7, 12; not necessary, 6-7; not profitable, destructive, 8, 15-16, 27, 28; origin and nature of, 116-18; ruling classes as cause of, *see* ruling classes: social structure as cause of, 11-12(2), 13-14, 49; *see also* ruling classes and states system, 8, 12, 117; *see also* balance of power; Concert of Europe; diplomacy; stupid, 6; and trade, *see* trade; Trevelyan and, 1-2; useless, 60; *see also* Crimean War; First World War; Korean War; Napoleonic Wars; Second World War; Vietnam; *also* peace
warrior class, warrior ethic, 11, 16, 28, 51, 53
Washington, George, 102
Weber, Max, 58
Wellington, Duke of, 36
Wells, H.G., 64
Wilson, Woodrow, 70, 71, 72, 102
Woolf, Leonard, 73, 84
working classes, workers, *see* 'people, the'

Yalta Declaration, 100, 103, 106